Deep Regrets :
The Story of One Man's
Journey

To: Duane

Chuck
Herring

Copyright © 2002 Charles Herring
All rights reserved.

ISBN 1-58898-734-5

Deep Regrets :
The Story of One Man's Journey

Charles Herring

greatunpublished.com
Title No. 734
2002

Deep Regrets:
The Story of One Man's Journey

PREFACE

We become who we are due to our choices as well as the events and people in our lives. Some events and people have more influence on us than others. My first beer was not nearly so defining as the Korean "Police Action." Fellow soldiers with whom I trained and fought were more influential than the girl I took to the prom. I am a fortunate man. I was blessed with the most wonderful wife a man could hope for; my parents imbued my early life with love and guidance; my children, and theirs, have taught me wisdom and another dimension to love. From my comrades in arms, I learned about courage, loyalty, unselfish heroism and a bond of friendship that has lasted over time and distance. From those with whom I worked, I learned skills, the value of doing something right even when it took longer and more effort. From my close friends, I learned the value of trust and fidelity to heart-held beliefs. My deepest thanks to all of you!

I originally began this as a "war story" about the sacrifices made by the soldiers I knew, but realized that others had done this and better than I ever could have. As I wrote I learned that what I knew the most about was myself and how I became what I am today. I wanted my children, my grandchildren and their progeny, to have a sense of the past that might enable them to avoid making some of the same mistakes as I have, in the future. I want the reader to understand how love and loyalty condemn us to be vulnerable. I am the center of this story, not its hero. I am here warts and all. I offer this story with a profound sense of humility about an ordinary man.

ACKNOWLEDGMENTS

I want to thank my wife, Mary Ann, who has supported me throughout the long ordeal of my journey through life and this book. My sons, Chuck Jr. and Bill took time from their extraordinarily busy schedules to read an early draft, and give me some beneficial criticism. (Finally got back at dad) Thanks also to my dear friend Alex Maxwell, who provided many insightful comments, and brought his usual superb editing skills and heartfelt enthusiasm to this wonderful story. Thanks also to Paul Kukuk who knew how to start my computer. A special thanks to Richard Trone, author of My Lemonade Days, and to Penn V. Rabb Jr., author of Tomahawk and Peace Pipe whom I served with during the Korean War, and whose encouragement spurred me on.

I also want to thank the folks at greatunpublished for their help and support while I demonstrated a lack of education in using the computer and following their formatting procedures.

To all those who helped me on this long journey.

Chapter One

It was cold and snowy in Alabama that December 29th in 1950. This was the day I was inducted into the United States Army. My Mother, accompanied by my little sister, Letha, had driven me to the train station in Birmingham. When we arrived at the train station, a hard-nosed recruiting sergeant, who was yelling at all of us young men, greeted me. He was saying things like, "Okay you squirrel tails, you're in the Army now, so kiss your mama's good-bye, and get in line, and we have a war to fight."

Mom and I embraced with big tears rolling down our cheeks. She said, "You be a good boy, and write me as soon as you get to Camp." I assured her that I would do so. My little sister didn't realize what was going on, but she started to cry, because mom and I were both crying. It was a terribly emotional time for all three of us. I was nervous, they were scared, and none of us knew what was ahead for me in the Army. But I knew that I had to go. The Commies had already taken over China and Korea down to the 38th parallel. They were now trying to turn the rest of Korea into a godless communist nation.

There were twenty of us boarding the train who had been inducted into the Army on this day. We were all nervous; not knowing what was ahead for any of us in the Army. Their moms, dads, sweethearts, or their wives were seeing off all of the others. It was a very difficult time for some of the men, because they didn't have anyone to see them off. They huddled together talking tough, and shivering from the cold.

When it was getting time for the train to pull out, the sergeant yelled, "Okay, get aboard." We all loaded into our assigned car, which, was filled with smoke, and a strong odor of alcohol. From the behavior of some of the men there, you could tell that they had been drinking.

As the train was pulling out, headed for Fort Smith, Arkansas where we would take basic training, I looked out of the window and could see my mom and little sis waving goodbye to me from the platform. Mom was talking to the recruiting sergeant about something. Later when I heard from mom, she said she had asked the sergeant if I would be okay, and said that he told her, "Oh yes, " I would be in the very best of hands." He told her that our Army takes good care of its young men.

During our travel to Fort Smith, the twenty of us young men became quite well acquainted with each other. There was one guy in particular that I liked right away, a young kid from Pell City, Alabama. His name was Sam Edwards. Sam was really handy with a deck of cards. He said that he had been raised in a family that played poker on a daily basis. He taught me a few card tricks during our trip, and, more important, he taught me how to play poker. When the troop train pulled into the station in Fort Smith the next morning at dawn, we were all groggy eyed from lack of sleep. A drill sergeant came through our car yelling, "Okay you mealy mouth whipper-snappers, its time to rise and meet your maker! Up and at 'em, we have work to do

When the train came to a halt, and the steam boiling from underneath the train simmered down, we were escorted off the train and onto an army bus. On the bus we met another screaming sergeant yelling, "Okay, load 'em up, you mama's boys. We're on our way to your new home for the next sixteen weeks. This is where you will meet God. You may smoke if you want too."

When we arrived at Camp Chaffee, the Basic Training facility outside Fort Smith, the bus stopped at the front gate. An MP [Military Police] entered the bus and said, "Welcome to Camp Chaffee. You will all depart from this bus. Another one will be arriving shortly. You are to load onto it for your destination here at Camp Chaffee, and the best of luck to all of you." Those were the kindest words we had heard from any army personnel since we left Birmingham.

We all off loaded from the first bus, and had to stand in the cold approximately twenty-five minutes before the other bus arrived. It was in the middle of winter! Man, was it cold! Some of the men didn't have winter coats on like a few of us did, but we all welcomed the sight of the other bus arriving to pick us up. We didn't know where it would be taking us.

After loading into the bus, the driver announced that our destination would take about fifteen minutes. If we wanted to smoke, we could do so!

We were driven to a large group of barracks buildings. Each building looked just like the one next to it. The driver was right about the time. It took every bit of fifteen minutes but the bus wasn't nearly as warm as we had expected it would be.

When we arrived in front of our designated barrack, another screaming sergeant greeted us. "Okay, lets go men, we don't have all day". We were told to enter the first barrack where we were each assigned to a bunk. We were told to leave all of our personal belongings next to our bunk. We were then told that in about 30 minutes we would be escorted to the mess hall for breakfast, our first Army meal, and man were we hungry.

The sergeant was right. It was every bit of 30 minutes before a corporal came in yelling, "Okay, fall out in front of the barracks, we will be going to the mess hall for chow." Every meal, from then on, was referred to as chow.

As we all tried falling out into rank and not knowing how, this screaming corporal instructed us how to do so. It must have looked terribly funny to anyone watching. To those of us who were new recruits, it was anything but funny.

When we were all lined up facing the corporal, he gave an order saying, "Right, face," meaning for us to turn to our right. Before he ordered us to march, he had told us that we were always to start marching on our left foot. That basic concept was one of our first instructions in learning how to march together as a unit. As a group, we caught on to the business of marching fairly quickly.

He then yelled, "Forward March."

When we arrived at the mess hall, which was approximately 150 yards from our barracks, we were instructed to halt, fall out and get in line for chow. As we entered the mess hall we had to pass by a young medic, who was handing out a pill for us to put into our coffee.

He said, "This pill is known as saltpeter, and the effects from it will diminish a male's sexual appetites for the first few weeks of basic training."

The food was terrible. It was nothing like mom used to make. The only food that I was able to digest for the first couple of weeks was peanut butter sandwiches. A peanut butter sandwich was the only thing that would stay on my stomach. I would just throw up the rest of the army food, as soon as I ate it. However, I like the taste of peanut butter. As a young lad going to school in Alabama, my mom used to make a peanut butter and banana sandwich for my lunch. So I had no problem eating peanut butter. I still like it.

When we had finished eating chow, we were escorted to the supply house where we were issued our basic training clothes. Our first issue was a barracks bag to hold our equipment and personal possessions. Surprisingly, we were all issued the sizes we requested. To expedite our movements, if anything didn't fit, we could later exchange it, for one that did fit. I didn't have to exchange anything, because everything fit me very well, even the shoes.

Our next instructions were to report back to our barracks, take a shower, and change into our fatigues. The clothing known as fatigues would be our daily dress while in basic training. When we arrived at our barracks, our bedding, towels, and footlockers were at the foot of our bunks

Some of the young men were very reluctant about undressing before a group of other men they didn't know very well. We were men, who until the day before had been total strangers. However, after a few "kind" words from our sergeant, we were persuaded to change and get ready for our first drill.

We got dressed after our showers, and our instructor

proceeded to teach us how to make our bunks, the Army way. When he finished with his instructions, he pulled a quarter out of his pocket, and flipped it up into the air, and let it bounce off the blanket on the freshly made bunk. As long as it bounced about six inches up from the blanket, it signified that the bunk had been properly made. Of course, when the instructor did it, the quarter bounced the required six inches. There were some that had problems making their bunks up to meet the army code.

We were then shown how to fold our socks and how to properly shine our shoes. They even had to show us the Army way to hang our clothes on the rack. The coat hangers had to be placed three fingers apart. The instructor completed the orientation of our clothing and then we were instructed to fall out for a little close order drill, which consisted of standing at attention, followed by a series of about faces, right and left faces, parade rests, and finally, to falling out. It didn't take us very long to learn this lingo. We were ordered to go back into the barracks, and change into our summer uniforms, and fall in again out in front of the barracks. We were told to go back into the barracks, change into our winter uniforms and fall out again in front of the barracks. Before falling out again we had to hang up our uniforms properly. What a workout that first day turned into. I changed clothes more times than a Broadway chorus girl. At the final falling out command, we found we liked that one best of all, which we were happy to do at the end of this first day.

The first night in the barracks was strange. We were all exhausted and our brains were overloaded, so we expected to fall asleep almost instantly. Though having a common bond, we were sleeping with strangers, or at least trying to. The night sounds of farting, belching, snoring, coughing, the occasional sleep talker, some sobbing, all combined with the adrenaline still charging through my veins, to rob me of my rest. Reveille came far too soon.

After two weeks of Army indoctrination we were assigned to individual companies in which we would start our basic combat training. Out of the twenty young men that had been inducted into the Army with me, only one of them was assigned to the same company with me. That person happened to be my friend Sam Edwards, the one who had taught me how to play poker on the train. Our orders were to report to Company "C" - 10th Medium Tank Battalion for the next sixteen weeks. We were cautioned to expect the unexpected

Our company, "C", consisted of four platoons; each platoon was made up of four squads. My friend Sam and I were both assigned to Squad Three. Our squad leader was Bobby Johnson, a young man from Cat "O" Mills, Texas. He was tall and lanky, spoke with an easy Texas drawl, and had worked for the postal service. We guessed that his government job had given him a leg up on us. The first week consisted mainly of attending classes, learning the different insignias, and what they stood for; from the three stripes of an NCO, [meaning non-commissioned officer] to the Five Stars worn by a top General of the Army. We were taught how to tell time the military way. O–four hundred meant 4:00 AM. And 1300 meant, of course, 1:00 PM. We were also taught how, and when, and whom to salute. We were also taught," when in doubt, salute anyway!"

We completed the classes, were issued a steel helmet, an M1 rifle, an ammo belt, a water canteen, and a bayonet. We finally began to feel like soldiers. They taught us how to break down our weapons blindfolded, how to oil and to keep our weapons clean. We were taught how to defend ourselves in hand-to-hand combat and how to kill the enemy with just a bayonet. We learned how to sneak up on the enemy from behind and cut his head off with a piano wire. The Corporal had been right when he told us to expect the unexpected.

Our field training was very hard duty. We would go on 10-mile hikes with a full 50-pound pack on our backs, which didn't include the weight of our weapons, steel helmet, and ammo. On the first hike, after about a half a mile of hectic hiking in the snow, we felt like taking some of the equipment off, and leaving it beside the road. But, of course, we didn't, because we would have been punished for losing government property. It was still awfully heavy, even for a former football player like myself. Some of the guys didn't make it. Exhaustion took a heavy toll on our ranks. Those recruits who collapsed had to be picked up, placed in an army ambulance and carried back to the hospital to recuperate. The weather made our march nearly unbearable. On another day, we marched at 10-degrees below zero. The rutted roads and rocky terrain we marched over were tortuous, slippery and hard as cement on the cold days, but slippery and mud sucking on wet days. We had only marched about five miles that first day before darkness approached. We were halted and instructed to pitch our tents right there and spend the night. Our food was brought out to us by truck.

We managed to pitch our tents, and dug a trench around them so that the water would drain away from us in the event it rained. We had just finished the trenches when a loud explosion of thunder blasted out of the sky, and heavy bolts of lighting flashed before our eyes. The lightening was striking trees all around us. This wasn't the enemy attacking us; it was Mother Nature. A torrential downpour began. Within minutes it was obvious that the trenches that we had dug around our tents were all in vain. The water flooded us out. Our wool blankets became soaked and heavy. We had nothing dry to cover up with during this cold, wild and woolly, wet night.

Before morning the temperature dropped to well below freezing. Icicles were hanging everywhere. Our clothing was soaking wet and we were chilled to shivers. Our platoon leader returned from a briefing with the brass, and said, "Get ready to move out. Trucks are coming out to pick us up, and take us back to Camp." These were welcome words – words that came to us directly from "brass" heaven. At our barracks, we all welcomed a nice, long hot shower and a shave. What a terrible experience that night had been. I'll never forget how cold I was in that wet, freezing tent.

I didn't have a lot of the problems that some of the men experienced, because I was in very good physical condition when I got to Camp. I had been an athlete in school and had worked as an Ironworker before entering the army. The rest of our training consisted of crawling under barbed wire in mud, while live ammo was being shot over our heads. We were cautioned not to raise our heads above ground level. That I am writing this assures you, I did not!

During our training we were taught how to march and how to parade on the parade grounds. I was elected to serve as a platoon guide. A platoon guide is the soldier who carries the American Flag during parades. I was selected because of my previous experience with the Alabama National Guard, and because I was the tallest guy in the Platoon. In the evenings we were allowed to go to the PX and buy 3.2 beer. We'd sit around B-Sing. This beer didn't have much of a kick to it, but it served our needs. It afforded us the opportunity to relax a little and develop friendships with our fellow soldiers.

After about ten weeks of basic training, everyone became somewhat resigned to our duty. However, there were a few men who would do anything to get out of the army. This one kid, Andy Biastock, a real hillbilly from way back in the Ozark Mountains of Arkansas, reminded me of Andy Griffith's character in the movie "No Time for Sergeants."

Our Andy would always volunteer for latrine duty, cleaning the toilets and showers. One day our First Sergeant came through our barracks to inform us that our Company Commander would be along shortly to perform an inspection. The Sergeant wanted his men to be prepared. Andy wanted so badly to get out of the army that he put peanut butter in the bowl of one of the toilets. When the Company Commander saw it, he asked Private Andy B, "What the hell is that, Private?"

Andy stuck his hand down into the toilet and picked up some peanut butter with his finger. He licked it, and said to the Commander, "I don't know, Sir, but it tastes like shit to me."

The Company Commander came completely unglued. Within a week, Andy got what he wanted – he was presented with a Section Eight discharge from the army: Unfit for Duty. Actually, I regretted losing him, as he may have been the right guy to have in a tight situation with an imagination like that.

Another time a kid named Bobby Arco wanted to get

out of the army so badly that he went into see the Company Commander, and told him, "Sir, I am a homosexual and I cannot guarantee being able to control myself around some of these beautiful naked men in the shower." In those days, homosexuality was completely unacceptable to military life. Bobby was also presented with a Section Eight discharge, even though he wasn't a homosexual.

During our remaining weeks of basic training, we were sometimes allowed weekend passes. Most of us would go into Fort Smith, rent a hotel room for the weekend and party. We would really have some wonderful parties in that old, run down hotel. But one thing was for sure; we had better be sober when we reported back to Camp the following Monday morning. There were some very lost weekends enjoyed in Fort Smith.

I didn't mind KP duty [Kitchen Police] as much as I did standing guard at some motor pool location all night long. On guard duty there would be no one to talk to, and it was very hard to stay awake while standing guard. Elvis Presley received his basic training at Camp Chaffee. Elvis, it was rumored, had an advantage over us while he was standing guard. He had access to Benny pills that would keep him awake all night long. The rest of us didn't even know what Benny pills were in 1951.

I was invited to attend Officers Candidate School because of how well I had scored on some tests. I declined the offer to attend OCS, because at the time, I wasn't sure if I wanted to remain in the Army or not. Even though the army considered me worthy of becoming an officer, I never received a single promotion while I was stationed at Camp Chaffee. I've always thought that a little strange. I was officer material, but they didn't add a stripe to my sleeve as an enlisted man. Maybe they were bothered that I declined their offer to accept an appointment to OCS?

The final day at Camp Chaffee finally arrived. Everyone in Company "C", except for me, received orders to report to their embarkation points in the United States. My orders were to remain there at Camp Chaffee to serve as a range instructor, teaching new recruits how to correctly throw a hand-grenade.

During basic training, I had qualified as a hand-grenade specialist. However, to make me an official instructor, I had to attend classes for four weeks before being sent out into the field to teach the new recruits how to throw a grenade, safely and properly.

Throwing a hand grenade is not like throwing a baseball. One must be alert at all times before throwing a grenade. If not thrown properly, one could suffer the consequences, which might consist of blowing off a hand, a foot, killing another soldier or killing oneself. After all, the Korean War hand grenade had been designed for only one purpose, killing people when it explodes.

The standing position is the first thing we taught. The soldier stands upright with the grenade in his right or left hand, depending on which arm he uses to throw things. Holding the grenade next to his chest, he then pulls the safety pin out with his other hand, while being careful to hold the lever down with his throwing hand. When the pin comes out, the grenade is armed and ready to explode. With the pin removed and the lever held down, the grenade is not dangerous. However, before the grenade is thrown, the soldier must release the lever. The lever is, of course, the mechanism that starts the fuse inside the grenade burning which, seven seconds later, causes the grenade to explode – thrown or not! Still holding the grenade with the lever down, the soldier reaches back with his throwing arm. The soldier's non-throwing arm is extended approximately 45 degrees to his front, for balance. Once he is sure he has solid footing, he releases the lever of the grenade, just as he steps forward, using the full force of his body, he throws the grenade as far forward as he possibly can throw it. The soldier then immediately falls to the ground for his own protection. Neither I nor my trainees ever lost any limbs, lives or digits.

I remained at Camp Chaffee until October 15, 1951, when I was issued orders to report to Fort Lawton near Seattle, Washington. Fort Lawton was a major embarkation point for troops going to the war in Korea.

Chapter 2

Before reporting to Fort Lawton, I was given a 10-day furlough. On October 15, 1951, I left Camp Chaffee and hitchhiked to Kevil, Kentucky, on the outskirts of Paducah, Kentucky. My folks were living in Kevil at the time, because my Dad was employed as an Ironworker on the construction of the H-bomb plant in Paducah. Dad got me a temporary job working with him for the week I was there, so I'd have a little extra money in my pocket. The day I left Kevil was a very sad day for my mom and dad because they knew this might be the last time that they would ever see their son alive. We were all in tears as I set out on the road for Washington State.

As it turned out, a friend of my uncle was in Paducah visiting him and his family. His name was Les Magnus. Les and my Uncle Raymond, my mother's sister's husband, served together in the Seabees during World War Two. Les and his wife offered me a ride with them as far as Omaha, Nebraska. I would have to take the train out of Omaha for the rest of my long journey to Seattle, but at least I could ride to Nebraska with family friends. I did part of the driving on the trip to Omaha. They wouldn't take any money from me to help pay for the gas. Les said, "Chuck, we had to go back home anyway. We were happy to have you come along. It was nice to lend a hand to one of our soldiers"

We arrived in Omaha about six o'clock in the evening. Les and his wife dropped me off at the train station and we said our good-byes. I went inside and bought a ticket on the train to Seattle. The next train for Seattle wasn't due to leave until that night at eleven. I sat down to wait out the five hours until the train was called. As I was sitting in the station lobby, reading a copy of Reader's Digest, a very pretty young girl approached me, and said, "Hi, soldier, do you have a long wait for your train?"

I said, "Yes, my train leaves at eleven."

"Would you like to go with me to the roller skating rink?"

I said, "Sure," and away we went.

We introduced ourselves, and when we arrived at the skating rink, she introduced me to some of her girl friends. I skated with them until it was time for me to go back to the depot and catch my train. This very lovely young woman drove me back to the train station and let me out.

As I thanked her for her hospitality, she smiled at me from the front seat of her car and said, "Take care of yourself, soldier." As she drove away, I realized I hadn't even kissed that girl goodbye. Today, I'm sorry to say, I don't remember her name, but I wish I could. I vividly remember those few hours on skates in Omaha, Nebraska. I've often wondered what ever happened to that pretty young woman who will never know how much her kindness had meant to me.

The train trip from Omaha to Seattle was two days long. The first morning I really was in need of a bath and a shave, so I asked the conductor if the train would be stopping any time soon. He said, "When the train arrives in Lincoln, we'll have a thirty minute scheduled stop while they drop off a few cars." I asked him if I would have time for a bath and a shave and he said, "Yes, if you hurry."

As soon as the train stopped, I jumped off and ran to find a barbershop in the train station. The barber let me use his shower, and then he gave me a shave. I was ready to get back on the train in twenty minutes. When I went to pay, the barber didn't even charge me for the shave or the shower. I thanked him and ran back to board the train. (How times have changed!)

When I got back on the train I found a girl sitting in my seat. She said, "Oh, I'm sorry. Is this your seat? I said, "Yes, but it's okay if you want to sit next to me." She told me she was on her way to Sun Valley, Idaho to go skiing. As the Midwest rolled by outside the window, this young woman and I got better acquainted. Before too long, she leaned over and kissed me. We smooched until she had to change trains a few hours later. She gave me her home address, and asked that I write her. I did write to her a few times while I was in Korea, and she responded. It never went anywhere, but the memory is still good.

It was the middle of the night when the train pulled into Union Station in downtown Seattle. It was snowing. When I got off of the train, I went over to the M.P's station, and they directed me to the place where I would be catching my bus for Fort Lawton. I don't know what came over me that night as I was walking toward the bus, but I felt as if I had been there before. Even though this was the first time I had ever been to the Pacific Northwest, I really felt at home,

When the bus arrived at Fort Lawton, I got off and reported directly to my assigned barrack where I was issued my bedding. I immediately set about preparing my bunk. When I finished, I went to bed and slept long and hard. It had been a tiring trip.

While waiting for my orders to depart from Fort Lawton to a destination that was still unknown to me, I was issued a pass to visit Seattle, and the surrounding area. As I was walking down 5th avenue in Seattle, I stopped in at a little tavern named the Drift Inn. It just happened that it was happy hour, so I drifted in for a glass of beer. I had no idea that this simple act would change my life forever. It was Friday, November 16, 1951. I was nineteen years old.

I ordered a beer and was soon asked to join a group of young people at a nearby table. Sitting at the table was a young girl named Mary Ann. It was love at first sight. We almost immediately began exchanging dreams for the future. I had never met anyone like Mary Ann. She was shy, but forthcoming with her thoughts. She was quiet, but very warm and amusing. We laughed and giggled through a pitcher of beer and then another. I had never been as comfortable with a girl that soon after meeting her, as I was with Mary Ann.

On this very evening, I felt I had everything to lose if I

didn't act right away. I blurted out, "Mary Ann, will you marry me?" Much to my surprise, she shyly accepted. I was filled with joy and wondered if we were crazy. We were, of course, but I'm even more joyful now after fifty years of marriage. I am still crazy about her. She has crazily stood by me all these years. Yeah, we were crazy and still are in our own private way.

That afternoon in Seattle, we both seemed to simply accept our destiny. Mary Ann and I saw each other every day for the next four days. Those were magical days for a nineteen-year-old kid from Alabama. Mary Ann and I became very well acquainted learning about each other, our families, friends, dreams and desires. I knew, in my heart, that we were going to be together for a long time, if and when I returned from active duty alive. Before I departed for Korea I had the pleasure of meeting both Mary Ann's mother and brother. But then, I finally received orders to depart from Fort Lawton, on November 20, 1951.

On the morning of November 21, 1951, all military personal that had orders to report for duty in Korea departed from Seattle International Airport for the Far East. Before departing, I had time to call Mary Ann and say good-bye to her. I promised I would return and we would get married.

On Thanksgiving Day our group arrived in Tokyo, Japan. We were immediately escorted to the mess hall, where we were delighted to find that a wonderful Thanksgiving Dinner had been prepared for us. It had been a long trip and we were all feeling homesick and lonely. It was the first Thanksgiving away from home for most of us. I still remember that turkey and those mashed potatoes enjoyed so far from home.

After a few days in Tokyo, we received orders to report to our outfits. My orders were to report to the 45th Division situated on Hokkaido, Japan, which is one of the four main islands that make up the nation of Japan. Hokkaido is just north of the main island of Honshu. After arriving at the headquarters of the 45th Division, I was assigned to Company "G," 179th Regiment. I was given the option of being assigned to an artillery company or an infantry company. I elected to join an infantry unit.

Before meeting with my Company Commander, and our squad leaders, I was issued new clothing, and a weapon, an M1 rifle. The guys in Company "G" really gave me a warm and hearty welcome. They were really a great bunch of guys. I began to pal around with some of them almost immediately. In the evenings, we would go out and browse around the nightclubs. We had some good times. One of the guys that I hung around with was a guy named Dan Blocker. (Later, after we returned from the service, Dan played Hoss Cartwright on the TV series Bonanza). Dan & I became very well acquainted during our service in the Korean War. He shared with me some wild and woolly stories about Hollywood. He encouraged me to go to Hollywood, and attend Hollywood drama school on my GI-Bill, when I mustered out. Dan was a Master Sergeant with "F" Company. He was a very fine, well-educated person. I'm still saddened by his untimely death of complications following gall bladder surgery at the young age of forty-three, on May 3, 1972. His death was caused from staph infection.

When it came time to go into combat, the 45th Division settled on a place called Yongdungpo, south of Inchon and east of Seoul, Korea, for our base of operations. About a year before we got there, the 1st Marines, commanded by General "Chesty" Puller, had come through Yongdungpo on their way to recapturing the city of Seoul, the Capital of South Korea,

We arrived at this God-forsaken place in mid-December 1951. We settled into our quarters, "air-conditioned" tents, though it was winter, and we immediately resumed our training, while awaiting orders to proceed with our first combat mission. Our training consisted of much of the same type of training that we had received in Japan before arriving in Korea. Hiking up the steep mountains with heavy packs, climbing over big boulders and then doing it all over again; all of these were very arduous tasks for most of us. However, the brave lads I served with showed no signs of regret, despite the occasional "not again" accompanied by expletives deleted. These men (who were mostly just boys, like myself) trained hard and served well, because they were training for a cause they all believed in,

Freedom! Soldiers training and waiting for combat, who have then engaged in combat, will truly understand these wonderful men and what they went through for their belief in and loyalty to, their country. It is for those who have not soldiered, and for these young men that I have written these memories. They were dedicated Americans and I was, and am still, proud to have been among them.

After long, exhausting days, we would take refuge in the tents that were provided and spend the evenings reminiscing about home, our loved ones and the things we missed so much back home. As Christmas quickly approached, we experienced a deep loneliness. We were young, scared, and, we were a long way from home. This was the first time that any of us young recruits had ever been away from home on Christmas. It was a very tearful time indeed. For many of those wonderful men, it would be their last Christmas here on earth.

On Christmas Eve we all sat around a big bonfire in our company area, singing Christmas carols, and opening Christmas presents that we had received from our loved ones back home. We had our beer rations, and some of the guys had received well-packed and carefully wrapped bottles of whiskey from home. We all made the best of it without being surrounded by family and friends or having our special girl with us. I missed home, but I also missed Mary Ann a lot. We all had our special Christmas song that we enjoyed. Mine was the old Bing Crosby favorite, White Christmas. I learned later that more people have purchased and listened to that song, sung by Bing, than any other song ever recorded. It's still my favorite. We all longed to be home with our loving families to share the warmth and security of their love. But as we sat there singing, we realized that we were in Korea and we were at war. We were cold, frightened and lonely.

We all celebrated New Years Eve together in a similar manner as we had Christmas Eve. There was, however, one big exception. Special Services staged a USO show for our company. It wasn't a Bob Hope show, but it served its purpose. There were dancing girls, and Spanky, the kid from the "Our

Gang" comedies, was the master of ceremonies. Spanky was great. So were the USO dancers. At midnight we shot off fireworks and started singing Auld-Land-Syne. About 0200 we went back to our tents and slept for the rest of the night. Our Company Commander was very kind. He allowed most of our company to sleep in on New Years Day. A few of the guys were less fortunate; they had to stand guard duty. I wonder how many of them went to sleep standing guard duty that night.

For the remainder of January we had lots of free time on our hands. The boredom of waiting weighed on us like the world on Atlas' shoulders... We filled our time with lots of reading, and wrote letters home. Johnny Trotter, Robert Lakie and I were able to scout around the hillsides of Korea and take some pictures. However, the cold, snowy weather didn't let up. There were some days when we were literally bombarded with heavy snowflakes. It was raw and cold on the Korean peninsula that winter.

Sometime around the first of February, we received orders to proceed to the front lines where we would finally engage the enemy in combat. Our means of transportation were our own two legs. We learned what it meant to be footsloggers or infantry. So, we packed up and started marching toward an unknown destination, which turned out to be our hell on earth. Korea's rugged terrain made marching a very tortuous task. Camp Chaffee had been a walk on Broadway compared to this agony in Korea.

Someone estimated that our march was about twenty-seven miles up hills and down into valleys, all through the blanketing snow. We knew that we were headed for hell; we didn't know hell was so cold and we weren't sure we would be coming back. The snow continued to fall, making walking even worse. At night we would pull off into a field, and pitch our tents. We only had candles to burn for light. Candles were considered a rarity and were extremely valuable, because the army didn't supply us with candles. We received them from our loved ones back home.

I must say that the army did provide us with plenty of

hot food, and saw to it that we received our incoming mail. It didn't matter that the mail was a month old, as long as we had something to read from our loved ones. It would boost our morale for days. We needed that, badly.

We marched for fourteen days on the trail, to be exact. This indicates just how hard the march was – we only averaged a mile and a half a day. When we finally arrived at our destination, the Company that we had been sent to relieve greeted us. They had all the bunkers cleaned out for us. When they departed, they took the same route back that we had taken to get there. However, they were headed back to the rear, and we were going forward to the front lines. We knew we were going the harder direction, but they had been there.

After we had settled into our bunkers, we could see our planes bombing the enemy on the mountainsides way off in the distance. The enemy was holed up in deep caves on the mountainsides. Unless a bomb landed directly in front of a cave, the enemy would remain safe from any explosion. I thought it was a terrible waste of munitions

February, even though it was the shortest month of the year, seemed like it would never pass. The days seemed long but the nights were even longer. Everyone was extremely tense, excited, fearful, but also filled with sadness. Some of the men in our group walked around like Zombies. Others exhibited strange behaviors, setting up strict regimens of seemingly useless activity, twitching uncontrollably, mumbling. Of course, the anxiety of not knowing whether you are going to live or die did could cause many people to act strangely. I easily sympathized with those who were having a tough time, because I, too, was scared to death of dying.

Chapter 3

March 1, 1952, was a very cold day in Korea. Through aerial reconnaissance, our company received information that the enemy would be approaching our zone in a short time. My squad was selected to secure an outpost located approximately 1000 yards beyond our company area. Our assignment was to secure the outpost and try to capture as many prisoners as possible.

We were instructed not to leave until dark. As darkness fell upon us, we moved out, determined to accomplish our dangerous mission. There were eight of us in the squad: Sgt. Charles Stone, Private Robert Lakie, Private Darling P. Shipes, Cpl. Cleo Duncan, Sgt. Arnold Davis, Cpl. Tex Trobridge, Private Erwin Knope, and myself, another Private.

As we walked toward our assigned outpost we were cautioned about the land mines that another squad from our Company had placed a few days before. They had placed markers near the mines so that we would know where they were and could avoid stepping on them. Markers or not, I was still very nervous about being blown to bits by one of our own mines, in the dark.

When we reached the outpost, we found that it consisted of four bunkers with only room enough for two of us in each bunker. We immediately took up our assigned positions. Erwin Knope was my bunker mate. Erwin, a young man of twenty-two, was from Wyandotte, Michigan. He was one of the finest people that I have ever known. I have thanked God so many times for letting me know and serve with this wonderful person during that awful war. Erwin was a handsome, loyal, honorable, trustworthy, and caring person. He cared deeply for his country, for his fellow man and for his family. We had become the best of friends during our training.

Erwin never went to a regular school. I never knew why he didn't attend school and never asked him I guess I thought that was too personal a thing to talk about. However, his efforts in life exceeded any formal education that any school in the land could have offered him.

One day sometime before this outing, our entire company had been sent out on maneuvers to the top of Old Baldy, which was a well-known hill, where lots of lives were lost on both sides during the ebb and flow of the war. While eating chow, Erwin and I were chatting about home, wondering what our loved ones were doing, when Erwin reached into his backpack and pulled out a letter he had received from his girl friend back in Wyandotte. To my surprise, he handed it to me and asked me to read this letter to him.

I said, "Oh, no, Erwin, I don't want to read your mail."

"Chuck, I can't read or write."

I was a little shocked, but I proceeded to read his letter to him. After I finished he asked me if I would mind reading all of his letters for him and maybe write a few in reply. Of course, I told him that I would be happy to do that for him. We became even closer friends from then on, because I learned so much more about him, his girlfriend and his family, all from reading those letters to him.

As we were standing guard inside the trench that was attached to our bunker at the outpost, that night seemed to grow even darker and colder. The darkness made it difficult for us to see anything, until the moon peeked out from the clouds for a moment or two. As we stood in the trench watching the clouds go by and listening for any unfamiliar sounds, we became sleepy. I suggested to Erwin that we take turns trying to get some shuteye. He agreed. I told him I would stand guard first and he could sleep for a few hours. I told him I would wake him if anything unusual happened. As I was standing there shivering in the darkness, I could hear water flowing down below. Our

DEEP REGRETS : THE STORY OF ONE MAN'S JOURNEY

bunker was adjacent to the steep embankment that bordered a river. Even the water sounded cold that night as it flowed past our position.

Charles Stone, our squad leader, crawled over to our bunker to ask if I had heard any unfamiliar sounds. I remember saying, "No!"

Then Stone
said, "I hope you're right, because Robert and I thought we had heard sounds like Korean talk. You know, 'garbo-garbo' kind of stuff.

He asked that I wake Erwin, and then he cautioned me to stay alert. Approximately fifteen minutes later, Erwin said, "Chuck, I think I hear voices that sound like Korean talk." I also heard them, but it was very difficult to see or hear anything as we stood there in the cold darkness at this outpost, both of us straining our ears to listen in the darkness.

Suddenly, all hell broke loose. Gunfire erupted all around us. Looking out of the trench where we were standing, we could see the silhouettes of the enemy slowing approaching our bunker. It was not until later that I realized just how noisy a firefight can be. My first thought was that they had probably killed our comrades in the other bunkers and were now coming after us. Erwin and I were scared beyond belief. The intensive training that we had received had been nothing like facing the enemy for real. I told Erwin to jump over the bank and try getting back to our outfit. Erwin took his rifle and rolled over the embankment and disappeared into the darkness.

It must have been too dark for the enemy to see me standing there alone in that trench, but I could see three of them slowly approaching me. This was first time I'd every faced the actual enemy. I was shaking very badly, scared and shivering there in the nearly pitch black, cold Korean night. When they were only about ten feet in front of me, I open fire with my BAR (Browning Automatic Rifle). I was so frightened that I must have concentrated my fire on only one of the Koreans, who was standing to the extreme right of me. I must have hit him ten times before he fell. For a moment I thought I was firing blanks. When he eventually did fall, the other two moved around to the back of our bunker. One of the Koreans climbed in through an opening and was now inside the tiny bunker with me. He turned on his flashlight and pulled the trigger of his burp gun. Fortunately, the gun jammed. I opened fire on him, and watched him fall. The third solider turned and began running away. I managed to fire a few shots at him, I think I may have hit him, but I wasn't sure. I'll never know.

Before long I could see some of the other enemy soldiers approaching me. I was out of ammo, because Erwin, my BAR assistant, had taken the ammo belt with him when he jumped over the embankment. I had no alternative. I had to jump over the steep bank myself.

I landed heavily and awkwardly on a big rock, which was protruding up out of the water. When I did, I ruptured the tendon in my right ankle very badly. The water was very cold and I was still very scared, but somehow I managed to escape limping and falling upstream on that damaged ankle.

As I looked back, I could see one of the Korean soldiers throwing hand grenades down the embankment. He must have thought I was in the water just below him. But I wasn't. I was hobbling up the stream away from the enemy as fast as my injured ankle would carry me.

I was even more scared, if that was possible, than before and was shaking badly, when all of a sudden something very strange happened. A warm, very welcome feeling that I had never experienced before suddenly came over me. There in the middle of the night, wading in that cold stream on a swollen ankle, I suddenly remembered a dream I had had the night before. A voice in the dream said, "Have no fear, God is with you, and He will take you through this war." Down at the center of my soul, I was warm in spite of the chill that engulfed my body.

I continued to move upstream, trying, as best that I could on an ankle that was quickly swelling more, to get back to my outfit. I was alone and scared. I was soaking wet, and very, very cold. I knew I was hurt, but strangely enough, at first, I hadn't felt any pain whatsoever. Several yards farther along the streambed I somehow managed to climb back up the steep embankment. But when I reached the top, I could hear enemy voices. I got very confused. What were these enemy soldiers doing so close to our company area? I nearly strangled on my fear.

Later, I was told, several of the enemy soldiers had crept in close and had cut our communication lines. But as I lay there on that riverbank, freezing, scared and hurt, I could only think about getting back to my unit. I scrambled back down the embankment and continued my tilted wading in the river, trying to find a spot far enough ahead so that I could climb back up the embankment without being seen by the enemy.

I did find a spot with a gradual incline where I was able to worm my way up and continue on to my outfit, if I could find it, if it was still there. As I made my way along, that warm sensation again came over all of me. I felt as if I were in a balloon floating alone. I was still upright and moving, although I had felt no pain for a while. But, after some distance, my right foot began to ache, and then throb, and finally, it began to hurt like nothing I had ever experienced. The throbbing pain increased with every step until it became completely unbearable. Finally, exhausted and in terrible pain, I tumbled to the ground and nearly passed out from the agony in my ankle.

I made several efforts to get back up on my feet and continue toward my unit, but I wasn't able to do so. I had no crutch of any kind for support. I had no choice. I could lie there and die, possibly be captured, or I could start clawing my way to safety. I began crawling along the ground, propelling myself forward with my hands and my one good foot. My ankle was so swollen it was nearly busting out of my boot and the pain had become a lion eating off my foot.

I was crawling along on the ground and looked back at where I had just been and saw that I had crawled through that minefield we had crossed on our way to our forward position. Only this time I couldn't see the markers. I didn't even know I had been crawling in the minefield. It seemed to me that God had walked me through that minefield. I began to cry and pray at the same time. I knew that no one could walk through a minefield and live to tell about it. The only words I can think of to describe the feeling that came over me at that moment was that I was not alone and God was protecting me. It was a feeling of spiritual peace. I was no longer frightened and I was no longer anxious. I knew I was going to survive.

I realized that I was getting closer to my unit when I encountered the barbed wire that we had positioned in front of our company area. We had gone around the rolled up barbed wire on our way to the forward position. On my return trip, with a terribly swollen ankle, I had no choice but to go through the six-foot high roll of barbwire. When I got into the middle of the barbed wire, I started yelling out to my comrades for help and to keep from getting shot by "friendly fire."

I identified myself over and over and when I heard Tommy Duarte's beautiful American voice yelling back at me saying, "Hold on Chuck. We're on our way," I breathed a silent prayer of thanks to God for His help and for allowing me to have such wonderful comrades.

Three soldiers, Tommy Duarte, Robert Skillen and Fred Thompsen, rushed to my side, picked me up and carried me to the first-aid station. My foot was swollen so badly the Medics had to cut the boot off. They gave me a shot of morphine and the pain began to simmer down. My Company Commander and platoon sergeant Joe Gray came in to check on me and get a report. But first, I asked them if Erwin or any of the others had gotten back yet?

My heart sank when I heard Joe Gray say, "No one got back except you, Chuck."

Then he began asking questions about what had happened out there. I briefed him on what I had seen and what I had done. His, "Good job, soldier!" made my heart soar for a moment until I remembered that my buddies were all dead. I turned my head and wept silently. Sergeant Gray put his hand on my shoulder and instructed the Medics to have me immediately flown by helicopter to the hospital at the rear.

Lying in the litter strapped to the side of the helicopter, I thought my foot was going to burst. It was swollen to about the size of a small watermelon. The pain was so bad I wanted to die. The Medics removed me from the helicopter as soon as we landed and rushed me into the hospital. Two Army nurses, one a male and the other a female, were standing by to care for me as soon as I was in the emergency room. They immediately placed icepacks on my foot to reduce the swelling. They could see that I was really hurting bad. They did everything that could be done to make me comfortable. The male nurse instructed the female nurse to go to the narcotic cabinet and bring in a hypodermic syringe with morphine. She quickly went to get it. When she returned with the morphine, he administered a dose of the painkiller. The pain diminished almost immediately. A few minutes later, he administered another shot that put me to sleep. I don't know how long I slept but it seemed like a long time. I awoke very slowly. I felt groggy from all the medication I had received.

I began to get my senses back. I had to know what had happened to the rest of my squad. I also remember asking myself, how I could have gotten through the firefight, and the journey up the stream, the mine field, all of that barbwire and received only a small scratch on my right hand. Then my foot began to assert itself with increasing intensity.

As I was thinking about that, a nurse came into my room and asked how I was feeling. I remember asking her for another shot of morphine, and she said, "No problem."

First, she took my vital signs, but said that she would return shortly. When she returned a few minutes later, she had a hypodermic syringe with morphine in her hand. While she was administering the morphine, she asked if I was hungry. I told her that I was very hungry. She said that she would have a tray sent in with some food. About thirty minutes later a couple of Korean girls, who worked in the mess hall, came into my room rolling a cart with food on it. I must have really been hungry, because I remember eating everything on that tray. I was eating when the nurse came back into my room and asked if, when I was finished eating, I would like to have a shot to help me get some sleep. I told her that I would like that very much.

The next morning, a doctor and nurse came in together. They checked my vital signs and asked how I was feeling. I told them that in fact I was feeling much better, but I also knew that as soon as the morphine started to wear off, the pain would return. Before he left, the doctor instructed the nurse to give me another shot of morphine. She went to get the morphine and an aide rolled a cart in with my breakfast on it. I almost finished it before he left the room.

I had just finished eating when a Lieutenant Colonel and a couple of news reporters from the Stars and Stripes Newspaper came in. The Colonel introduced himself, and began asking questions about what had happened out there at the outpost.

I told him my story but before he could get a word in, I asked him about the rest of my guys there. The light Colonel hesitated a moment, but told me what he knew.

Charles Stone, who was our squad leader, was shot and killed, probably at the outset of the fighting. Robert Lakie, who was with Stone, took some of Stone's blood and smeared it all over his face and played dead. He survived. Cleo Duncan was shot and killed. Darling P. Shipes, who was with Cleo, was captured and taken prisoner. (After the war, Shipes was released and sent home) Tex Trobridge and Bill Davis were stationed in a bunker to the far right of the rest of our bunkers and they both survived. In fact, they were never even approached by the enemy.

My friend Erwin Knope apparently lost his balance when he jumped over the embankment and was subsequently killed by the enemy. My thoughts for these wonderful men have never vanished from my memory. I still think about them and the sacrifice they made for the cause that we all believed in. War is filled with pain and longing and always terrible sorrow. Those men who died out there in the frozen mud trenches were good men. They were robbed of a full, rich life, dying as they did in their late teens and early twenties.

The Colonel also informed me that the soldier, the one

who climbed into the opening of our bunker with a flashlight and a gun, was a Korean Lieutenant. I hadn't killed him, but only wounded him. He was the first prisoner taken by the 45th Division. The Colonel told me that this prisoner had revealed lots of useful information that turned out to be very beneficial to our side. Because I had caused this prisoner to be captured, I would receive a $25.00 reward and five days of R&R in Japan.

After the Colonel and the reporters finished with the interrogation, they took a few pictures. As the medication was wearing off, my foot began to throb. I called for the nurse to bring me another shot of morphine. This would be the last time I would need any morphine. Icepacks would serve the purpose from then on.

I remained in the hospital for three and a half weeks, until I was nearly completely recovered from my injuries. I was released from the hospital and sent back to my outfit. During the time I was away from my outfit, Company "G", had been engaged in several more attacks from the enemy. It's sad to say, but I sometimes thought that my friends had become almost callous to the loss of our buddies. But when I returned from the hospital I was greeted by a warm, hearty welcome from all the guys in the outfit.

Two weeks after being back with my unit, orders came down for me to pack up and get ready to leave for my five days of R&R (Rest & Recuperation) in Japan. Lots of the guys gave me money so that I would have a very enjoyable time, and so I could bring them back some whiskey. They were such a great bunch of men. There is something about being together in a crisis that makes men draw closer together and share not only the past but also makes the present last a lifetime.

Company G received several newcomers from the States as replacements for those we'd lost in combat. They were a great bunch of guys, but that original group was irreplaceable. I never really got as close to the newbies.

My goal as a soldier became, to make it through this war and, after being discharged from the army, marry Mary Ann and finish my schooling through the GI Bill. I had dreams of attending the University of Alabama, and playing football for Coach Bear Bryant.

With Deep Regrets, I was reluctant about writing the letter to Erwin's parents, informing them of how their son was killed, but I had to do it. This was one letter that was very difficult for me to write. How do you tell someone about how their loved son was killed, *Especially when he was their only son?*

I knew that by now Erwin's parents had received a telegram from the Defense Department informing them that their son had been killed in action. However, the telegram would not have explained how he was killed. As I was writing the letter, I kept thinking about how my parents would react if they received a letter from a buddy of mine, describing for them how I had been killed. It was a very hard task for me, but it had to be done. It was very difficult to describe the terrible events surrounding his death that seemed so trivial to anyone who had not been there. They appreciated my telling them of Erwin's going for help for his fellow soldiers in the face of the enemy, of his last words. Some time after I had returned to the states, Erwin's parents came to visit Mary Ann and me. We loved that man and grieved together, engraving his memory on our souls.

Erwin Knope killed in action in Korea.
1930-1952

Chapter 4

DETERMINATION

On the evening of May 25, 1952, in a dream, a voice seemed to say to me that I would be wounded in both legs, prohibiting me from ever playing football. On the next morning our squad received orders to go out that night and try to capture some prisoners. For the first time we were all issued bulletproof vests. They had just been issued to our unit that very day.

At the battle zone, we could see the enemy out in front of us and before they had a chance to open fire on us, I threw a white phosphorus grenade, cremating one of them. Apparently, one of the enemies had thrown a hand grenade at us at the same time I had thrown the white phosphorus grenade. The grenade landed to my left, exploded and wounded three of us. I was wounded much more severely than the other two. At the time of explosion I didn't feel any sensation of pain from the fragments of the grenade that had penetrated my body. I fell to the ground, and tried to get back up, but wasn't able to do so. This is when I realized that I had been seriously wounded. The white phosphorus (aka a"willy peter") grenade that I had thrown, cremating one of the Korean soldiers seemed to have panicked the enemy into a retreat. That made it easier for the Medics to remove our wounded, including me, without enemy interference.

Fragments of the grenade had hit all over my body. Had I not had the bulletproof vest on, I would surely have been killed.

The bulletproof vest prevented any shrapnel from penetrating my heart. However, I began to try digging out the sizzling metal fragments from both legs. The muscles in my legs were shredded and raw in the open air. Suddenly the Medic's were dragging me over the sharp, jagged rocks, away from further danger. In the red pain I had what seemed to be an out-of-body experience. From somewhere above, I could see them dragging me over the rocks and I didn't think I wanted to go back into my body. Wherever I was seemed peaceful and warm. Dad and our home seemed to be there as well as my girl friend, Mary Ann, in beautiful Seattle. Every thing was in color. I had never seen so much beauty in my life. The feeling was a sensation that I had never felt before. Then they began shooting me with morphine, and I returned to my body. The pain diminished a bit but I wanted to go back to where I had found so much solace.

After the Medics had dragged me back far enough from the battle zone, all of my buddies gathered around me. I remember hearing David Gibson saying, "Chuck, you have got the million dollar wound, you will be going home." He grabbed hold of my hand, and said, "Goodbye, ole buddy, take care of yourself and think of us." I was placed in an army ambulance and taken back to an aid station somewhere in the rear. I was taken inside this large tent where the wounded men were, as soon as we arrived. God, I was living inside an envelope of sheer pain. I was thirsty; my tongue was dry and swollen. I begged for a drink of water. The Doctor said that I had lost too much blood, so, I couldn't have a drink. He did swab my tongue with a wet sponge. I remember crying, begging for something to relieve the pain. They then began to inject me with morphine.

As I was lying on this army cot, crying and not knowing what they were going to do with me, they rolled another wounded solider in and laid him on the cot next to me. I saw that his arm was hanging down, just about to fall off of his shoulder. It seemed to be held by just a few bloody threads of muscle. He was screaming. I shut my mouth; it looked as if he had been hit with a hand grenade.

Several of us were rolled out of this aid station about an hour later and loaded onto a helicopter. A major military innovation of the Korean War was the use of helicopters—nicknamed "eggbeaters," "whirlybirds" and "airdales." They were used for transport, re-supply, evacuation, rescue and observation. The helicopter has changed modern warfare. No longer do we have to expend time and energy getting to the battlefield, but now we can nearly immediately get to where we're needed as well as to remove the wounded to aid stations for something more than immediate emergency treatment.

This helicopter was from a U.S. Air Force air rescue squadron. As soon as it landed, four of us wounded GIs were carried forward for extraction to a hospital at the rear. We were strapped down on the floor of the helicopter, so that our litters wouldn't move around during flight. There were no doors on this chopper. I guess it was for easy access in and out of the chopper with the wounded. The four of us wounded soldiers were really in pain. We were all crying, and hoping that we would be arriving at the hospital soon, so that we could be taken care of.

Twenty five minutes later, we landed in a wide-open space, next to some large army tents used as hospitals. There were other choppers landing as well, bringing more wounded GIs in from the nearby war zones of Korea. There must have been several severe attacks that night, because there were about 100 wounded GIs landing at the same time we were. The roaring whop, whop of several helicopter engines, ambulances, the driven dust and confusion were frightening. As we were being off-loaded into the hospital, the voices of the medical personnel shouting instructions during triage added to the seeming chaos and din. They laid the 4 of us on the floor of a hospital tent. We must have been lying there 30 minutes before anyone came to our aid. They picked our litters up and immediately put us onto gurneys, and rolled us into a surgical room. I later learned that they had been working short handed, and that's why it took so long before they came to pick us up. They had been compelled to fly in more doctors and nurses and equipment from other nearby hospital units to help with the overrun of the wounded.

I really admired those doctors and nurses; they were really working their butts off. It all reminded me of the movie *Gone with the Wind*, in that scene in Atlanta, Georgia, when Scarlet was asked to help with the wounded.

That night as we were being flown to this hospital, strapped down in the helicopter with our pain, I was looking outside at total darkness, when I saw a little white cloud that seemed to be flying alongside us. It appeared to be an angel flying with us, as if to say, I am your guardian angel. The strange events that occurred for me all seemed to have occurred when I was in the agony of suffering. I have only heard of two rational explanations for them. The first was that the mind shuts out the pain and reverts to protective memories to escape the pain. The other was offered to me from a cynical friend who said that some drugs could make you "think you're talking to God." I don't know what I think, but am surely glad they happened.

From Korea, I was flown to a hospital in Osaka, Japan. There it was determined that my chances of ever walking again without the aid of crutches, or braces of some kind, were very slim. I spent several weeks in the hospital at Osaka, undergoing Psychological Therapy. The mind docs were trying to enable me to accept the fact that I might never walk again on my own.

During my stay in the hospital at Osaka, I received the best of care. All of the members of the hospital staff were very encouraging. They also saw to it that I got plenty to eat. One day a Red Cross worker approached me, and wanted to know why I hadn't written to my parents. It seems that my parents were really worried about me, since receiving the telegram from the war department informing them that I had been wounded in action, yet they had received no word from me about my condition. The Red Cross worker would not leave until I wrote my parents a letter. When I finished writing the letter, she assured me that she would see to it that it got in the next outgoing mail. She stayed with me for some time. It was very comforting, having a nice, pretty girl to talk with. Her name was Alice, and she was from Montgomery, Alabama, so we had a lot in common, because Montgomery is where all of the Herring's originated.

About a week later, I received a letter from my Dad.

He said, "Son, don't you worry about anything. I will take care of you the rest of your life, if need be."

I remember responding to his letter, and thanking him for his concern. But I assured him that the Army would take care of me. I knew that my Dad was having a hard enough time as it was, because he was supporting my mother and three sisters, who were just kids in school. I had made an allotment out to my mother, but it wasn't very much. It was the best I could afford at the time.

I was well cared for during my stay at the hospital in Osaka, Japan even though I didn't receive any massages like I did the first time I was wounded, but I was bathed everyday. One day after I had received my daily bath, and had finished eating my lunch, I was approached by a Lieutenant Colonel accompanied by a lieutenant and a master sergeant. The master sergeant was holding a box with something in it. They all stood at attention, and the colonel said, "Private Charles Herring, we are here to present you with a Purple Heart, and an Oak Leaf Cluster to the Purple Heart, and to assure you the President of the United States sends his condolences. The United States appreciates the sacrifice you've made." The sergeant extended the box he was holding and opened it. The colonel took a Purple Heart medal from the box, and pinned it to my pillowcase. The lieutenant and the sergeant both were standing at attention, saluting me. The colonel stepped back, and saluted me. I saluted him back. The Colonel then told me that I had been recommended to receive the Silver Star, when I arrived back in the States. I wasn't aware that they were sending me back to the States until the Colonel had mentioned it in telling about the Silver Star.

Every hour that I spent in the hospital, I was well taken care of. They would dress my wounds and saw to it that I got whatever I requested, like writing paper, cigarettes, and pain medication. In those days we were allowed to smoke in a hospital room. There was one nurse that came to work everyday at 5 p.m. She would care for me during her shift. Her name was Judy. She was a 2nd Lieutenant. She would always wheel me out in a wheelchair to the movie house. She would stay with me until the movie was over, and then wheel me back to my hospital bed. Judy was a very pretty girl from Dallas, Texas. She only had 6 months to serve before her enlistment was up. She told me that when she received her discharge, she was going to return to Dallas, and go to work for a large hospital in Dallas. Her future husband was already working at the hospital as a Doctor. He had just finished his internship.

Finally, the hospital staff decided that I be returned to the States for treatment, and be separated from the Army with a medical discharge. My doctor entered the ward, and said to me, "You are to be sent back to the States." There I would be cared for, but he laid it out straight. They didn't think that I would ever walk again. He seems to think that there might be a slight possibility that I may be able to walk, with braces. I didn't question his opinion, as I was so happy to hear that I would be going back home. After he left the ward, I started writing letters to all concerned. Then, I remember writing to Mary Ann, saying that it would be okay if she wanted to disregard our plans for getting married, because of my disability. This was another letter written *With Deep Regrets.*

On the day of my departure from the hospital in Osaka, Judy and the others came in to wish me good luck. Judy hugged me and gave me a nice long kiss. I think she may have fallen a little bit in love with me. But I knew that it was never meant to be. As the aide was wheeling me out to the ambulance, Judy walked along beside me. She had tears in her eyes. While helping me into the ambulance, she kissed me on the cheek. I wished her the best of luck when she got back to Dallas in her marriage to her boyfriend. She slipped a piece of paper into my hand, as the ambulance was pulling out. I last saw her standing on the steps of the hospital, waving good-bye to me, with tears rolling down her cheeks.

Riding to the airport, I opened the note that Judy had given me. It consisted of two paragraphs. "Chuck, I have come to realize that during our acquaintance, I have fallen in love with you and realize it is just a one way affair. I know that you are in love, and plan to marry your girlfriend in Seattle, Washington. How I wish that it could be me. I will have to go on with my life as planned, like you. Please write me if and when you feel lonely. I don't plan on getting married for a year or so after my discharge. I will never forget your cheerful smile. Here she included the address where she would be for the next six months, along with her address in the U.S. and a telephone number where she could be reached.

Love Judy."

I will never know what became of Judy since I never wrote her. I didn't want to complicate her life and I had to get back on my feet, quite literally, before I planned any future.

In the States, I was taken to a military hospital at Edward's Air Force Base in California. The hospital staff all warmly welcomed us. We received the best of care right from the outset. I finally worked up the courage and placed a call to Mary Ann in Seattle from a pay phone, but it turned out I didn't have enough money to pay for the 3 minutes. I explained to the operator that I had just arrived from Korea, and didn't have enough money to pay for the call. I remember her saying, "Go ahead and put in what you have."

This I did, and Mary Ann was really happy to hear from me. She wanted to catch a plane immediately and come to be with me in California. I told her that I would not be at this hospital very long, and for her to wait until I arrived at my final destination, a destination that I didn't know at the time. The telephone operator did not cut in and say "your 3 minutes are up." Mary Ann and I talked for at least an hour, and when I hung up the phone, the money I had put in to call Mary Ann was returned to me in the phone slot. (The operator had to be a wonderful person; I have always wanted to thank her for her kindness. Here I have.).

After a few days at Edward's Air Force Base, I was transferred to a military hospital in Mobile, Alabama. I was to be there for only a few days. I immediately called my Mother in

Bessemer, Alabama informing her of my whereabouts. She said that she and my little sister (Letha) would be catching the next bus to Mobile. They arrived the next morning. We embraced and shed a few tears of joy together. We spent the entire day together. They left that evening and caught the bus back to Bessemer. My Mother was a delightful lady. Later she told my dad, "That short stay was well worth the trip just to see my oldest son." [Bless her heart]

The next morning, I boarded a plane for the ambulatory, even though I didn't qualify, headed for Camp Gordon, in Augusta, Georgia. This is where I would receive all of my surgery and therapy in the weeks ahead. The staff at Camp Gordon was very professional. They worked with me hour after hour trying to make me feel comfortable. They were genuine and kind people. I got all that I needed from them and they got all my respect and gratitude.

When I had been there a month, they still held little hope of my ever walking again without the aid of an apparatus of some kind. They explained that my right foot had become what is known as "a drop foot," something like a person who has had polio might experience. I couldn't hold it up or control it. I would always have to wear a brace. A piece of shrapnel had gone through my right foot, cutting a tendon, causing me to have what they call hammer toes, which can never be straightened. The muscle in the calf of my right leg was also severely damaged. The muscles in my left thigh were blown completely out of my leg, causing all of the nerves in this leg to become paralyzed. They still are today.

I will never forget the letter I received from Mary Ann, informing me that she would be taking her vacation from work on June 12, 1952. She also said she would leave Seattle on the morning of the 13th. The letter said she would be arriving at Camp Gordon on June 15. I was so thrilled. I could hardly wait for June 15th to arrive. Mary Ann arrived by train to be with me during my stay in the hospital. She was a great encouragement to me. Without her I don't think I would have recovered as well, or as fast as I did. The entire time that I was in Korea,

Mary Ann and I wrote to each other on a daily basis. Her letters always gave me hope.

There were times when I would receive 15 or more letters on a single day from Mary Ann; it took that much time for the mail to catch up with me. I always received more mail than anyone else in our Company. One day after I was released from the hospital the first time to rejoin my outfit, I was sitting in my bunker writing a letter to Mary Ann, when Sergeant Roy Thompson stopped by, and said, "Herring, how about you going and pick up the mail at the mail room."

I asked, in a joking tone, "Why me?"

He said, "Well, there are 33 letters at the mail room for our Company, and 32 of them are for you, so don't you think you should go?"

I said, "Oh, yes, sir. I guess I should."

Her arrival on the morning of June 16 was a beautiful day, not too hot, just right. Everyone on my floor knew that she was coming. They were almost as excited as I. That morning a male nurse assisted me into a wheel chair so that I could get to the shower and clean up for Mary Ann's arrival. Mary Ann had rented a room at a local boarding house, so that she would have a place to stay while she was with me. About 10 o'clock the nurse came to my bedside and told me that my girlfriend had arrived. I told the nurse to send her in. As I set up in my bed waiting for that wonderful moment, Mary Ann came walking in with a big beautiful radiant smile on her face. Her beautiful, long black hair sparkled. She was more beautiful than my memory or imagination. My heart rate must have been going 100 beats per minute. We embraced, and kissed our faces wet with tears of joy. My eyes got drunk on her beauty. I was so happy that she had come to visit me that I knew more certainly than ever; I wanted to grow old with her. She stayed with me all during the time of my surgeries. They still had not sutured my wounds and the muscles were still exposed. The doctors said that they wanted my wounds to heal from the inside out. Before long we decided that she would not go back to Seattle, but would stay with me until I was well enough for us to get married.

In my heart of hearts though I wanted to be with Mary Ann more than anything in the world, I was somewhat reluctant about getting married. Not that I didn't love Mary Ann, but I just wasn't sure what the final results would be from my injuries. I wasn't sure if I would recover well enough to get a decent job so that I could support a family. I certainly didn't have any money saved up. But those things didn't seem to bother Mary Ann. She seemed to think I had potential and trusted in us and our future.

If I was committed to restoring my life, and committed to the person that I had chosen to spend the rest of my life with, I knew that I had to get well. My educational background was only high school, plus I had served an apprenticeship as an ironworker through Ironworker's Local # 92. My last job, before going into the Army, was as an ironworker on the Veterans Hospital in Birmingham, Alabama. Atlanta Steel Erectors had been my employers. As an Ironworker, I would be able to make enough money to support a family very well. I just wasn't sure if I would be able to perform the work, physically.

I used to get out of bed and try to walk without the aid of any apparatuses. I would fall, but I always managed to get back up and keep trying. I did this time and time again. I also did a lot of praying. One day I was able to walk a little bit on my own and that gave me great hope. I continued on with the help of the therapists, day in and day out. Mary Ann took a job at a restaurant in Augusta. This caused me to become very jealous. Mary Ann was so beautiful and there she was, working in this Army town with all those other soldiers around her all the time. I knew that I had to get well as soon as I could, because I was afraid some other guy might take her away from me.

She told me, "Chuck, you don't have anything to worry about, because I really love you."

The doctors were all amazed that I was making such a speedy recover. However, they assured me that there was no panacea for my condition. I worked on until I finally did away with the crutches and braces and began walking on my own. I walked very slowly at first, but I continued to make progress slowly but surely. One day while the doctors were making their rounds in the wards, my doctor approached me, and asked if I was ready for a 30-day leave. Of course I said, you bet! Yes!!" So Mary Ann and I packed up and went to Bessemer, Alabama where my parents were living. We stayed with them up until the day we got married.

On August 16, 1952, Mary Ann and I were joined together in the bonds of Holy Matrimony at Saint Aloysius Church, at Bessemer, Alabama. *("Wherefore they are no more twain, but one flesh. What therefore God hath joined together, let no man put asunder." (Matthew 19: 6)*

After Mary Ann and I were married, there was a small reception in our honor at my mother's house. My Aunt Myrtie Oliver, from my mother's side of the family, was invited, but for some reason she wasn't able to arrive in time for the wedding. However, she and my cousin Myrene did arrive in time for the reception. Aunt Myrtie was a dear lady of our time. She was so happy to have made it to the reception. She said, "I was afraid that Mary Ann and you would have already left on your honeymoon before I had arrived." Aunt Myrtie was the mother of a dearly beloved cousin of mine, (Nellie Dean Oliver). Nellie Dean and I attended our freshman year of high school together. She was six months older than I was. We were very close. On August 8, 1950, Nellie Dean was fatally injured in an automobile accident. She was only 18 years old at the time of her death. Accompanied by her sister, Myrene, and a friend, Hilda Gibson, Nellie Dean had, only five days before that tragic accident, returned from a 5,875 mile trip through Canada and a large number of the States. I was genuinely happy that she and Myrene were able to be there.

Shortly after we had returned from our honeymoon we learned that Mary Ann was pregnant. We rented an apartment in Bessemer, because both Mary Ann and I thought it would be best for her to remain in Bessemer during her pregnancy. She would be close to my mother in the event she needed any help. After she had the baby, Mary Ann and the baby would join me at Camp Steward, Georgia. Meanwhile, Mary Ann went to work for Thompson and Street Construction Company. They were the General Contractor on the Veterans Hospital in Birmingham. It was the same hospital that I had worked on before going into the Army.

On May 12, 1953, Mary Ann and I received a precious gift from God. We were blessed with the birth of our oldest son (Edward). He was born at Bessemer General Hospital in Bessemer, Alabama. I wasn't able to be with Mary Ann during the delivery. When I knew the time was near, I called my mother and she informed me that our son had been born. I immediately requested a pass to go home. A 5-day pass was all that I could get. When I arrived in Bessemer, I immediately went to the hospital. My mother greeted me. Mary Ann and Edward were doing fine. I was so proud to be the father of such a fine boy.

After a couple of days, Mary Ann was released from the hospital. We went to our apartment and settled in with our beloved son. I called my Company Commander at Camp Steward, requesting an extension on my pass. My request was denied. I never did understand what the urgency was for me to return to Camp so soon. When I did return, I was informed that my orders had come though for me to report to the MP (Military Police) School, and I had to be there on that certain date, otherwise I would have to wait six months.

It was very, very sad day when I left Mary Ann and Edward on my way back to Camp. I felt like going AWOL (Absent without Leave). But Mary Ann encouraged me to return and to keep my chin up. She always encouraged me to do the right thing.

After completing six weeks of schooling, I was assigned to the Military Police, and to work with the CID (Criminal Investigation Division). I enjoyed the work immensely. Shortly after being assigned to the Military Police, I requested a 10-day leave, so that I could go and bring Mary Ann and Edward back to Camp with me. The leave was granted. I immediately called Mary Ann, informing her of my intentions. She was delighted.

When I arrived by bus, Mary Ann had everything packed, ready for our departure. I had just enough money to make a down payment on a used car. I went to a used car dealership in Bessemer, and bought a 1946 Fleetwood Chevrolet. The car looked good, but I didn't know anything about the mechanism. The used car salesperson was a real con artist, plus the fact I was very naive. I took the car for a test drive; it started up OK, and ran OK, so away we went.

Mary Ann and I loaded the car up, and proceeded toward Camp Steward. We had driven about 100 miles, the sun was sinking, and getting dark, so I reached to turn the lights on, and they wouldn't work. We had to pull off to the side of the road, and spend the night in the car. Did I ever kick myself all through that night? When daylight came, we continued on our trip. We stopped at the nearest restaurant for breakfast. Mary Ann changed Edward's diapers; and after finishing with our breakfast, we proceeded on our way. About 100 miles from Camp Steward, a loud noise started in the engine. I remember saying, "Oh no, what now?" I knew the next town was only about 10 miles ahead so; I drove as slow as I could without causing too much damage to the engine. I managed to drive up to a garage there that looked somewhat respectable. The loud noise from the engine sounded as if it would explode any minute. The mechanic, also the owner, who was summoned by the clamor of the engine, came out, and said, "Sounds like a blown rod or piston."

We rolled the car into the garage where he began to inspect it. He came into the waiting room where we were, and said, "The engine threw a rod, and I don't have one in stock. I'll have to call my supplier. It will take all day for delivery and another day to install. We had no choice but to authorize the work. He said, "The total cost for parts and labor would be $82.00."

But realizing our situation, he said he would reduce the cost by $10.00. We only had $110.00, and out of that we would have to pay for a motel for two nights plus food, and we would have to have money to buy gas for the rest of our journey to Camp Steward. I was really beginning to worry, so I placed a collect call to Monroe Herring, a cousin of mine in Montgomery, Alabama. I knew if anyone would have any money to loan us, he would. He offered to loan $50.00, and would wire it to the motel where we were staying."

What a relief!

After the mechanic completed the repair to our car, we loaded up, and away we went. I never exceeded 35 miles per hour. When we arrived at Camp Steward, I checked in with the First Sergeant, and I asked him if he knew of any place to live that I could rent for my family. He said, "There is a big farm house about seven miles from Camp, and there are some other military family's living out there." He gave me directions to get there. When we arrived, which was just in time, the landlord said that she had just one bedroom left, and we could have it for only $7.00 per month. However, we would have to share the bath with another couple, who had a baby the same age as our baby. They were very nice people.

We settled in our rented room, and carried on with our daily lives. I got up every morning, and reported in for duty. I really enjoyed the work that I was doing. Mary Ann said that I liked to play cops and robbers. I realized that it wasn't going to be easy going for Mary Ann. She was a young girl with a little baby. In those days there weren't any disposable diapers. They were cotton cloth, and first had to be washed by hand to remove the poop, and then put into a washer. When the cycles were completed, Mary Ann would have to hang them out on the clothesline to dry. Mary Ann quickly adapted to our new way of life. She was a real trooper.

Our stay at the farmhouse was only for a month. Next, we rented a one-bedroom house closer to the town of Hinesville, which fortunately was very inexpensive at the time. Money was very tight with us. There was a time or two when we had to pawn Mary Ann's silverware, a wedding gift from Mary Ann's mother. We were never able to get more than $10.00 for the set, but at least we managed to survive until payday. Times were very hard for us but they were happy times just because we were all together.

My enlistment was nearly up. I was scheduled to be honorably discharged from the army on January 10, 1954. On

November 30, 1953, I was eligible for a 10-day leave, so Mary Ann and I decided to pack up and go to Lenoir City, Tennessee where my parents were living at the time. Mary Ann and Edward were going to stay with them while I was waiting to be discharged from the army. Two of the tires on our car were getting bald, so I replaced them with two new ones. We packed everything into the car, and away we went. The sun was slowly going down, and we were getting pretty hungry, so we decided to stop at the next truck stop, which wasn't too far up the road. As we were pulling off to park, a loud noise started up in the engine, I knew it had to be another blown piston. Well I didn't have enough money to have it repaired, so I placed a collect call to my dad, and asked him if he would come and get us. My plan was to abandon this car. However, my Dad suggested that he could rent a tow bar, and would come to get us and tow the car to his place. I gave my Dad the name of the place where we would be staying.

He said, "It will probably take me about eight hours to get there."

After we had finished eating, we checked into a motel room that I had rented for the night. Mary Ann asked the question, "What have we done to deserve this?" We were both feeling pretty discouraged. The next morning about 5:30 a.m., my Dad arrived. He had driven all night, and he was awfully tired. We hooked the car up to the tow bar. We headed out of town, but not before we stopped at the truck stop and had breakfast. I drove most of the trip

We arrived at my parent's house exhausted from the trip. We parked our car on the street, in front of my parent's house. I unloaded the car while Mary Ann took Edward into the house and immediately started with his bath. Mary Ann and I had our shower, a bite to eat that my Mother had prepared and went promptly to bed, and slept very soundly.

The next morning, a Sunday, we all got out of bed and had breakfast that my mother had prepared. Mom was always an early bird. After we finished with breakfast we all got ready for church. My oldest sister (Betty) kept Edward while Mary Ann and I attended church with my mother and dad. This church was the First Baptist Church of Lenoir City. This was the same Church that I had gone to each Sunday while I was attending Lenoir City High School.

My leave was just about over. I would have to report back to Camp, which I hated to do especially since we would be apart. One consolation was that it wouldn't be for long. Mary Ann walked to the train station with me, which wasn't very far from my parent's house. Mary Ann and I embraced, kissed, and shared a few tears. It was a very difficult moment for us. I still get a lump in my throat just from the memory.

I called Arlo Miller, a buddy of mine, from the train station at Camp Steward, and asked if he would mind coming to the station to pick me up. I knew that he could check out a patrol car from the motor pool. Arlo arrived and took me back to our outfit. I had to check in with the First Sergeant, so that I could obtain quarters to stay in. Since I had been living off post, I had never been assigned living quarters on the base.

I got settled in, I called Mary Ann letting her know that I had gotten back to Camp safely. She thought that she was coming down with a cold. It had snowed just after I left Lenoir City, and was very cold. She was glad to hear from me. We could have talked for hours. But, I continued on with my tour of duty until the time of my separation from the army, which was on January 10, 1954. It was a very happy day for me, for soon I would be reunited with Mary Ann and my son.

On January 10, I had to go through the different processes of being discharged from the army. With my discharge, I received my mustering out pay of $400.00 they offered me a promotion if I would reenlist for another two years. I declined the offer; because this didn't make a lot of sense to me. I didn't understand why they waited until my enlistment was up before promoting me to a higher rank.

I boarded the train In Hinesville, Georgia for home, where Mary Ann and Edward were, with a light heart. Mary Ann was waiting for me at the train station in Lenoir City. The steam had not even stopped boiling out from under the car when Mary

Ann came running toward me with open arms. We hugged and held each other for what seemed a long time. Both of us were greedy with our kisses and filled with elation.

Chapter 5

Mary Ann and I talked about what we should do. I could have gone to work as an Ironworker, but I wasn't physically up to that challenge, just yet. I knew that she was getting homesick. So, we decided that we would go to Seattle and visit with her family. We made reservations to leave Knoxville, Tennessee, on the evening of January 22, my 22nd birthday. Mother and dad drove us to the train station in Knoxville, about 25 miles from Lenoir City.

We boarded the train that night with high hopes and many dreams. The trip was scheduled to take three days to Seattle, with a change of trains in Chicago after the first night. The rest of the trip was very pleasant until we were about two hours out of Seattle. At that point I was invited to sit in on a poker game in the club car. I had always been lucky at the game, my old army buddy, Sam Edwards, had taught me. I thought this might be a chance to increase our meager cash assets, so I anted up and started to play. I wasn't as lucky as I thought I might be. Before I knew it I had risked nearly everything we had. I did have enough sense to hold back enough money to buy Edward some milk before we arrived in Seattle, but I lost everything else. As I walked back to our seats I was filled with dread. I had to tell Mary Ann that we were completely broke. Mary Ann, as you might imagine, was more than a little upset with me as she had every right to be. I had been completely inconsiderate and foolish.

Mary Ann's mother and brother were at the station in Seattle to meet us. They were so happy to see Mary Ann and Edward. Mary Ann's mother (Helen) was a gentle and charming woman. And her brother Bill was really an okay guy. It was snowing in Seattle, and very cold. Helen and Bill had both taken off work to meet us. The first thing Mary Ann told Helen was that we didn't have any money without going into any details. I sure thanked her for that in my heart. I remember Helen saying, "That's okay, I'm sure Chuck will quickly find a job."

When we arrived at Helen's apartment, Bill assisted me with our luggage. They lived on the top floor of the apartment building. He was still living at home with Helen. After settling in, Helen prepared a scrumptious breakfast that consisted of scramble eggs and waffles. After we finished eating, Bill asked us if we wanted to go with him over to his other sister's house in the University District of Seattle. Mary Ann said that she would rather stay with Helen and bathe Edward and then put him to bed for a nap.

Bill and I journeyed over to his sister's house. It began to snow as we were traveling, which was fine with me, because I love the snow. When we arrived, Bill rang the doorbell, and Kathy, who was 5 years old, answered the door. Bill's sister, Margaret, was on the phone talking to Mary Ann. Margaret's husband, Howard, was in the basement working on a part for his boat. Howard was a commercial fisherman. They had two children, Kathy and Biff. Biff was only 13 months old, or six months older than Edward. Bill introduced me to the family, and we chatted for about an hour before leaving. Bill then drove around Seattle, showing me some of his hangouts (Taverns). We stopped at a couple of them and had a drink or two with some of his friends.

When we returned to the apartment, Mary Ann said that Margaret had invited us over for dinner that evening. When we arrived for dinner, Mary Ann and Margaret embraced and shared the hugging and kissing of Edward and Biff. Kathy was so excited to see her Aunt Mary Ann again. We all became acquainted, and after dinner the topic of conversation became the future. It was decided that we should stay at Helen's for a while, and then we were welcome to stay with Margaret and

Howard. Margaret and Howard both assured us that it would not be a problem.

While staying at Helen's apartment, Mary Ann and I decided that we would remain in Seattle. I would find a job and we would get our own place to live. I soon found out that it wasn't healthy or wise to live with in-laws. Even though we never had any disagreements, it was sometimes uncomfortable. We just needed our own privacy. I went to the train station and turned in our return trip tickets for a refund. I remember calling my dad to inform him of my decision to stay in Seattle. He was, of course, disappointed. He said, "I had a job all lined up for you, working at Y12 in Oak Ridge, Tennessee" Oak Ridge is one of the places where the atomic bomb was built.

Money was very tight. Had we not been able to stay with Mary Ann's mother and sister, we would have had to go on welfare. On February 1, 1954, I went to the Veterans Administration Office Building on 7th and Olive Way in Seattle. A VA doctor examined me. He told me that I would be notified of the results within a few days.

In the meantime, I continued looking for work. I checked in at the Ironworkers Union # 86 in Seattle to see if I could get a job through them. The Business Agent informed me that they didn't have enough work for their own members, and that they were not considering any out of town member of another Local. My home local was #91, Birmingham, Alabama. Construction work was very dismal in Seattle at the time.

I had already met some of Mary Ann's Seattle friends. One of them, Patsy Gibson, was an old high school friend. Patsy had married a guy that she and Mary Ann had known for a long time, George Bruno. George worked for Carter, McElroy & Johnson Inc. They were a Crosley and Bendix appliance distributor in the University District. They employed George as a shipping clerk.

One evening, I received a call from George. He told me that he was being promoted to inside sales, and he was wondering if I would be interested in taking over his job as shipping clerk. Of course I said I was very interested. The next day I stopped in for an interview with Jerry, George's boss. I was hired on the spot, and started to work the next day. George taught me the ropes. The pay rate was $1.50 per hour, 40 hours per week. I had a job.

Since I still didn't own a car, we rented a one-bedroom house within walking distance of Carter, McElroy & Johnson. Things were beginning to look up for us. We soon saved enough money to buy a 1949 two-door Ford sedan. Mary Ann's brother went with me to buy the car. He was a good mechanic. We drove around and checked the car out very thoroughly. It was a very pretty car, and we enjoyed it immensely. It was also in good working order. I didn't have to worry about another blown piston with this car.

The compensation that I was receiving from the VA every month, plus my wages, meant that we were able to manage pretty well. After three months on the job, I was given a fifty-cent per hour raise in pay. I was now earning $2.00 per hour and felt great about it. One day, after I had been working with the company for six months, Mr. Carter, the owner came into the shipping area were I was working, and said, "Well, Chuck, I have some bad news for you. We will be closing the Seattle operation down within a month, because we're moving the company to San Diego, California." He offered me a job with them in San Diego, and agreed to pay our moving expenses, if I would accept the job. If I didn't agree to move south to San Diego with the company, I would be laid off. Mary Ann and I discussed the pros and cons of the move into the small hours of the morning. I declined the offer. Mr. Carter paid me a month's severance pay and wrote a very nice letter of recommendation on my behalf.

We stayed in Seattle for a while, while I tried to find another job, but I wasn't able to do so. I became restless and was able to convince Mary Ann that we needed to return to my hometown, Birmingham, Alabama. I loved Seattle, and had hopes of returning someday. We would leave behind in Seattle some lifetime friends like Don and Jan Donnelley. They were a great comfort to us in times of our loneliness. Jan was with

DEEP REGRETS: THE STORY OF ONE MAN'S JOURNEY

Mary Ann when I first met them both at the Drift Inn Tavern in Seattle before I shipped out to Korea. Jan is gone now, and we have lost contact with Don. Jan will always have a special place in both of our hearts.

I mailed my resume along with the letter of recommendation from Carter, McElroy & Johnson to the Steel City Supply Company in Birmingham. They were the Crosley and Bendix distributors in Birmingham.

I rented a U-Haul trailer and hooked it up to our car. We loaded all of our stuff into it; hugged and kissed everybody good-bye and away we went. Mary Ann's mother, Helen, asked if she could come along with us as far as Torrington, Wyoming. Torrington was where Helen's own mother was living at the time. Her name was Katie. She was a feisty little old lady. I had the utmost respect for her. She was 89 years of age when I met her. Her only source of income came from washing and ironing clothes for other people. After she completed her ironing, she would hand carry the laundry, in a basket, to her customers. She'd often stop in at a nearby tavern and have a glass of beer on the way home. Katie was one heck of a person.

Our trip time from Seattle to Torrington had taken nearly two full days of driving. We stopped in Sunnyside, Washington to pick up a trunk of Helen's that she had left while she was living in Sunnyside in 1941. That was when Bill, Mary Ann, Margaret and Helen first moved to Washington from Nebraska. Helen's dad, Frank Hilderburg, was living there at the time. Frank had wanted Helen and the kids to move to Sunnyside to be with him, so that Helen could cook and care for him. After sizing up the situation, Helen said, "No thanks, Pop. I am going to Seattle, and find myself a job in one of the department stores." And that's exactly what she did. She went on to Seattle and never looked back. She worked at Graysons for a number of years before going to work for J.C. Penny. She retired from there.

Helen took us to dinner at a nearby restaurant the evening before we left Torrington, as a treat. We went back to Katie's house to settle in for the evening. Our plan of attack was to rise at dawn to continue on our journey. Departing was a tearful time for Mary Ann and Helen; they were full of heartache and sorrow at being separated. Helen did assure Mary Ann that she was doing the right thing; sticking by her husband. I will never forget her words. From her, they were high praise. She said to Mary Ann, "Your Charles is a good boy."

From Torrington to Lenoir City, Tennessee, our trip time took about three full days of driving. I wasn't able to drive very fast, because of the trailer I was pulling. Each day at sundown we would stop at a motel, and spend the night. And each morning we were awakened at five by our alarm clock. Edward was such a delightful child to travel with. He was 13 months old, and acted like a little man. He was a very cheerful little boy when he woke up in the morning. He was so well mannered when we took him into a restaurant. I've seen some kids that throw their food everywhere. Real messy. Not Edward.

After a long and tiring trip, and no air conditioning in our car, we were exhausted when we arrived at my folk's house. My mother couldn't get over how much Edward had grown in such a short time. It was evening, and mom had dinner already prepared. We spent that first weekend with my folk's, but on Monday morning we departed for Birmingham, Alabama. It was about a six-hour drive to Birmingham. The first thing we did was rent a motel room for the night. The next day we rented an apartment in an area known as Central Park, which is on the outskirts of Birmingham. It was actually between Birmingham and Bessemer, Alabama.

I checked in with Steel City Supply Company, the company I had sent my resume to from Seattle, and much to my delight, they hired me on the spot. The wages weren't much, but it was the best job I was able to get at the time. They promised an increase after a three-month "getting to know you" period. We stayed in our rented apartment for a month, but after the first few days we decided to look for another place to live. We found a house in a community named Beachwood, which was near the airport in Birmingham. We lived there a couple of months. Our next-door neighbor, Jack Campbell, worked at the US Pipe and

Foundry Company as a boilermaker. Jack and I became pretty good friends. I asked him to let me know when a job opening came up for a boilermaker, and he assured me that he would. Mary Ann and I weren't thrilled with the neighborhood in Beachwood, so we decided to look for another place to live. One of the guys that I was working with at Steel City Supply said that there was a little brick house next to his house, and that the upstairs was for rent. We checked it out. The owner of the house was a lady named, Mrs. Tucker, who lived in the downstairs part of the house. The upstairs consisted of just one bedroom, a small kitchen and, of course, a bathroom. It was small, but it suited our needs pretty well. Mary Ann really loved that little brick house. We made an offer to buy it, but Mrs. Tucker didn't want to sell. We continued to live there until I got laid off from Steel City Supply Co. The demand for Crosley & Bendix merchandise in the area apparently was not very high. Eventually, Steel City closed up shop completely.

Construction work in Birmingham was at a stand still. I had been promised I would be called as soon as there was some work. In the mean time, I placed a call to Mary Ann's ex-boss, Calvin Rutledge in Atlanta, Georgia. Calvin was her boss when she worked for Thompson and Street Construction Company during the construction of the Veterans Hospital in Birmingham. A friend of mine told me that Calvin was now in Atlanta, and that he was a superintendent of a large office-building project. I called information to get his phone number, and when I did speak with him, he assured me that I could go to work if I came to Atlanta.

So, I headed out for Atlanta, leaving Mary Ann and Edward in Birmingham until I could find a place for us to live in Atlanta. When I arrived in Atlanta, I went straight to the job site to find Calvin. He immediately made arrangements for me to start work. Since it was about quitting time for the Ironworkers, I left the job site to find a place to stay. I found a room at a boarding house. I checked in for the night, and went to bed very early. I wanted to be rested up for the next day. I, of course, was hoping to make a good impression with the crew.

When I arrived at the job site the next morning, ready for my first day on the job, Calvin greeted me with welcome, but unexpected, news. He told me that Mary Ann had called him after I left, and told him that Jack Campbell had called her about the job at US Pipe. Jack told Mary Ann that they were planning to shut down blast furnace #1 to do a complete overhaul. He told her that they would be hiring one boilermaker, and if I was still interested in the job, I should be there for an interview by 1:00 PM the next day. That was today. I thanked Calvin for his job offer, but I told him I thought we would be better off if I were to accept the job with US Pipe in Birmingham. Calvin understood completely and wished us well.

I left Atlanta about six o'clock that morning as soon as I gathered my things from the rooming house. Without that pesky trailer in tow, I could move right along toward my future as a boilermaker. It was only about a three-hour drive back to Birmingham. When I arrived in town I went directly to US Pipe to see Jack, without waiting for that one o'clock appointment. It didn't take me very long to find him. He introduced me to the job superintendent and I was hired immediately and told to report for work the next morning at seven. Jack explained that my employment would be considered temporary or just long enough to overhaul that one blast furnace. If the company was satisfied with my work, I might be considered for permanent employment. My probation period would be for 30 days. After that period, if they offered me a permanent position, I would have to join the boilermakers union. I started to work on January 10, 1955, and was terminated seven years later. I guess you could say it was a permanent position.

I couldn't wait to get home and tell Mary Ann the good news about my new job. Believe me, this was just what we needed. When I arrived at the little brick house, Mary Ann and Edward were upstairs. They were both very happy to see me and, believe me, the feeling was mutual. I suggested that we go out for a bite to eat, to celebrate my new job. There was a pancake house nearby that had just recently opened. I can't remember when waffles, sausage, and eggs tasted as good.

Chapter 6

This marked the beginning of a new chapter for Mary Ann, Edward and me. On my first day of employment at US Pipe I reported to work a full hour earlier than I was asked to report. I was very excited to have such a good a job. At seven o'clock I found my time card in the rack, and clocked in. I was now a workingman with a family and a good job. The first few hours that first day were mostly spent on orientation. Mike Gambel, the foreman for the boilermakers, escorted me around to the various stations that I would soon become familiar with, such as the first aid station, shower house, locker room, and tool room. The shower house was a facility where everyone was encouraged to take a shower before going home. Working around a blast furnace is extremely dirty work; especially during the time of realignment shut down.

I finished the orientation process just in time for lunch. I joined the other guys and ate my lunch. Jack Campbell introduced me to all the other employees that I would be working with on this job. They were a nice bunch of fellows. They all welcomed me with open arms. One of the guys, a fellow named Sam Smith, was serving in Korea at the same time I was. It just so happened that Sam had also served in the 45th Division, and he was in "F" company with Dan Blocker, (Hoss Cartwright). Small world. By the time I went to work in Birmingham, Dan had already made the big screen in Hollywood. First he had been featured in a movie called *Cimmaron City*, starring George Montgomery. From there he was cast in Bonanza on NBC.

After lunch, I was assigned to work with Sam for the balance of the shift. The work was very time consuming; sometimes the task would require two trades on the same project, such as a machinist, and a boilermaker. While the machinist would be performing his task, the boilermaker would have nothing to do, but remain on standby and vice-versa.

During the standby time on my first day, Sam and I became well acquainted. We began reminiscing about our time in Korea. I asked him if he remembered the incident that occurred one night, when "G" company was called up to relieve "F" company at the foot of old Baldy. The enemy had pinned down "F" company. We were called in to give them support. When we arrived, we were instructed to guard "F" company's rear flank. We lay there on the cold, wet ground for most of the night.

At dawn we were able to see what had taken place during this attack. Apparently the enemy had retreated sometime during early hours. At least we didn't see any of them at first light. Dan Blocker was the master sergeant of "F" company during this attack on his outfit. We started checking out the scrimmage line of "F" company and discovered that over half of his company had been killed during the night. I found a North Korean soldier lying in a trench filled with water. The soldier had been severely wounded, but still alive. I knelt down beside him and could hear him mumbling something, although I wasn't able to understand what he was saying. I was about to put him out of his misery by cutting his throat with my bayonet, when Dan Blocker stepped in, and said, " Hold on Chuck, let me finish him." I could see the anger and tears in Dan's eyes as he opened fire at this wounded soldier. He must have shot him at least 10 times before he was grabbed and ordered to stop firing by his company commander.

Sam said, "I remember the incident, but I didn't know that you were the person that had attempted to cut the North Korean soldier's throat." Sam was one of the "F" company survivors from that night of horror.

After I was wounded the 2nd time, and sent back to the states, I lost contact with Dan Blocker and most of my other buddies. However, I had been communicating with David

Gibson, from Detroit, Michigan. In Korea, he and I found a stray puppy and we nursed it back to health. It was to be our mascot, and hopefully would bring us luck. We couldn't decide on a name, so we decided to name it Gibher, (a combination of our last names, Gibson, and Herring, Gib-Her)

David survived the war. However, he had told me, in one of his letters, that one of our buddies, a fellow named Robert Ryan from Madison, Wisconsin, had been killed in one of the attacks on them. Ryan was a very nervous type of a person. I will never forget what he used to say during the times when we just sat around shooting the bull. "Chuck," he would say, "I know that I'm going to get killed here. I know I will never get out of this God forsaken country alive. These rotten sons-of-a-guns! Why are we even involved in this stinking war, anyway?" I guess just about every war has had the soldiers who have asked that very same question.

The 2nd day of my employment at US Pipe, blast furnace #1 was closed down. The air was shut off from the furnace so that it could cool down to a low temperature. After it cooled, we would be able to enter the furnace and start the task of dismantling it. There were four blast furnaces in Birmingham at the time. Furnaces #1 and #2 were located on First Avenue, where I worked and #3 & 4 were located in North Birmingham, which was about ten miles away.

The function of a blast furnace is producing pig iron. It wasn't until 1871 that someone discovered that using coke instead of charcoal could make pig iron. (This iron is called "pig iron" because the first-pour molds look very much like baby pigs. Coke is made from coal, but it produces more heat than plain coal)

We were able to start the process of overhauling the furnace when it cooled enough. It was a very exciting time for me. I was lucky enough to have a good job, and I was able to learn all the different functions of a blast furnace. I also had high hopes of being able to remain with the company after the completion of the overhaul. I knew I could prove to be a valuable employee.

When we started the overhaul process, the schedule was a killer. We were to do the work in two-12 hour shifts. When the overtime started, I worked three 12-hour shifts (36 hours total) before going home. I called Mary Ann after the first shift and told her not to look for me until the next day. I wanted to get in enough hours so that I would receive a large paycheck. We were paid time and a half for all hours over eight hours. My first paycheck was really a whopper. But believe me, I earned that money. I was really exhausted after working those three straight shifts without sleep.

I went straight home afterwards. Mary Ann had a wonderful meal prepared for me. After I finished eating and Mary Ann saw to it that I went straight to bed. I slept for twelve solid hours without waking. When I did, finally, awaken Mary Ann had breakfast all prepared for me when I woke up. I ate, then kissed her and Edward goodbye, and left for work.

After the overhaul of the furnace was completed, things got back to normal. We went back on a work schedule of eight hours a day, instead of sixteen. I was a little worried that it also might mean the end of my employment. But, I knew I had done a good job and I knew that I had made an extra effort to become valuable to the company. There wasn't anyone there who worked harder during those last few weeks. In a short time, I got the word. It was the consensus of the company, and of the men I was working with, that I remain on as a regular employee. I couldn't wait to get home and tell Mary Ann of the good news. When I did tell her that I was now a full time, permanent employee of US Pipe, I recall her saying, "Thank God. Now we should be able to get on with our lives."

And so we did.

My Veterans compensation – as a partially disabled veteran - and my weekly paycheck were coming in regularly now, so we decided that we would move into a little better neighborhood. We rented a two-bedroom, unfurnished apartment at Cherokee Gardens, which was located in a community named East Lake. Before moving in, we went on a little shopping spree. We bought only the necessary furniture that we would need at first;

which consisted of a hide-away bed for the living room, a 21" Philco television, a couple of lamps, and two end tables. For the bedroom, we bought a king-size bed and a nice day bed for Edward.

One of our neighbors, a guy we called "Happy" (last name forgotten) and his wife were an older couple. They were both always so helpful and cheerful to us. "Happy" was the nickname that we had given him. We owned a new two-door 1954 Ford sedan, which had a stick shift transmission with a clutch. Some of the guys that I worked with lived in this neighborhood, so we would take turns driving, an early car pool. When it came my week to leave my car at home, Happy would take Mary Ann and go for a ride while teaching her to drive. He was a very patient teacher and never got upset as I might have. I was never patient enough to teach her. Happy's wife would keep Edward during these driving lessons. And, by the way, Happy taught Mary Ann how to drive very well. She's still an excellent driver.

After I had been with US Pipe for one year, I was entitled to a one week paid vacation. Mary Ann's mom, Helen, called and said that she would be taking her vacation, and would like to come to Birmingham to visit. I made arrangements with the company to take my vacation during the time that Helen would be with us. When she arrived at the train station in Birmingham, Mary Ann, Edward, and I were there to meet her. She was so thrilled to see us, and we to see her.

We took her back to our apartment, and I remember her saying, "Oh! Mary Ann, I'm so happy for you. "Chuck has a good job and you three have such a nice place to live." That night we took Helen out to a nearby restaurant that had really good food. Helen and Mary Ann had salmon, and Edward and I had fried chicken. Those Seattleites like the taste of salmon.

The next day we took Helen on a tour of Birmingham, and its surroundings. Our first destination was Bessemer, Alabama, just a few miles from Birmingham. We wanted to show her the hospital where Edward was born, and the church where we were married. Bessemer was a town started by a fellow named Sam F. DeBareleben, who believed the town, would become one of the great industrial centers of Alabama. He named the town Bessemer after the English scientist who had developed the Bessemer furnace. This blast furnace, known as the "Bessemer Converter," was one of the first designs used to make iron into steel.

From Bessemer, we went back to Birmingham and drove to the top of Red Mountain. Red Mountain is where the statue of the Vulcan stood. After climbing the stairs to the top of the Vulcan, as the day was nearing sunset, we looked down on the city of Birmingham. There before us, we could see millions of lights, which stretched as far as a person, could see. Tall buildings with thousands of blinking windows, like groups of stars, rose toward the sky. The red, yellow, blue, and white neon signs winked off and on. The streets were filled with the lights of countless moving automobiles. It was a beautiful sight.

We could see a red glow in the sky far off in the distance. We could see the rows of smokestacks standing tall and red above the steel mills. I knew the workers were "pouring steel." White-hot sparks belched and showered from the great iron furnaces. We could hear and feel their sound, rumbling like thunder, shaking inside our bodies. For the time of the steel pouring, the noise from the steel mills was louder than the noise of the city. The Roman candle lights of the great furnaces died down and the thunder from the steel mills stopped. We could hear again the humming noise of the streets among the lights. At the time there were over 300,000 people who worked and lived in Birmingham, Alabama. Helen was very impressed with Birmingham. She said that one would have to see it to believe it. It was getting late and we were all getting hungry; so, on our way home, we stopped at the nearest restaurant and had dinner. Yup, salmon!

The next day of our vacation Mary Ann asked Helen what she would like to see while visiting in the south. She said that she would like to visit the city of New Orleans, and see some of the southern plantations that she had always heard about. So, we packed up the car and headed for New Orleans. Along the way, we stopped in and toured some of the plantations. This would be the first time that I had ever visited any of the old plantations and I was born in the south! It's almost a truism that people are frequently unaware of what is in their own hometowns that others will come to see.

At sunset we were getting pretty tired, so we stopped and spent the night in a motel. At sunrise the next morning we headed out for New Orleans. I found out one thing about my mother-in-law on that trip. She was a very consistent lady. When six a.m. came around, she had to eat breakfast. She was also ready to eat lunch at noon and dinner at six p.m.

We arrived in New Orleans, checked into a hotel to spend that night and the rest of the next day. During our short stay, we walked up and down Bourbon Street, which is the most famous street in the French Quarter of New Orleans. New Orleans was laid out in 1718 and became the capital of Louisiana four years later. The new capital building of Louisiana is now in Baton Rouge, and is the largest and, some say, the most beautiful modern building in the state.

Before leaving the state of Louisiana, we visited the area surrounding Lake Pontchartrain where Mary Ann's brother, Francis, had been stationed during World War Two. He was in the Navy, and served as a Frogman, with an underwater demolition unit. (Francis died in 1950). As we were leaving the state of Louisiana, we decided to visit my folks in Tennessee on the way home. Helen had never met my parents. She said that this would be a good time to do so.

I called ahead to notify them that we were on our way to visit. As usual, they were very happy to see us, and especially happy to see Edward, their only grandson. And they were also very happy to meet Helen, although my dad and Helen didn't see eye to eye regarding religious beliefs. Helen was Catholic, and dad a hard-shell southern Baptist. It made for some spirited conversations and confrontations.

My vacation was slowly, but surely, coming to an end. I had to be back at work on Monday. We only had a day and a half to spend with my folks before we had to start for Birmingham. Helen wanted to go through the Great Smoky Mountains, and see one of the wonders of the modern world, Clingman's Dome. At an elevation of 6,642 feet above sea level, the Dome is the highest point in Tennessee. Vistas from Clingman's Dome are spectacular. On clear, pollution-free days, views expand over 100 miles and into seven states. However, air pollution limits the average viewing distances to about twenty miles. Despite this handicap, breathtaking scenes delight those ascending the tower. It is a great place for sunrises and sunsets.

After leaving the Great Smoky Mountains, on our way to Chattanooga, we took some side roads, and toured some of the historical points of Tennessee. One of the places we visited was Lookout Mountain. Tennessee has numerous points of interest: historical, natural, and man-made. The many TVA lakes and United States Engineers lakes offer scenes of surpassing beauty and excellent fishing.

The next week I turned down quite a bit of overtime, because I wanted to spend as much time with Helen as I could before she had to return to Seattle. We sure did enjoy her visit. It was a sad day for all of us when we took her to the train station. She and Mary Ann, of course, shed a few tears.

After Helen's wonderful visit, we got back into the regular routine of our life. Happy continued to teach Mary Ann how to drive. When the time came for her driver's test, Happy went with her. Although she was a little nervous, Mary Ann passed with flying colors. She was really proud of herself. She enjoyed driving to the shopping center to shop for groceries without me. Every Friday she would drive to the parking lot at the plant and I would meet her with my paycheck. All the wives did that in those days.

Life seemed to be so rewarding at this time of our lives. Edward was such a happy little boy. I remember one day when he was playing in the back yard of our apartment with a rubber ball. The ball rolled into a hole. He didn't get upset, as many children would. He just said, "Well. Ball in hole," in his cheerful little voice, knowing dad would fetch it out for him. Mary Ann became pregnant again during our stay at Cherokee Garden Apartments. We decided that it was time to move on, and buy a nice house. We checked out all of the new housing projects that were being built in the area. We found a 3-bedroom house in Roebuck, which wasn't too far from where we were living. We both fell in love with this house, even before we looked inside. It was new, and had hardwood floors. We contacted the real estate agent and she agreed to meet us at the house.

When we arrived, the real estate lady was already there. The address was 337 Pat Avenue. The inside of the house was nicely laid out. It had a large living room, dining room, and a large kitchen; [just what we needed] the bedrooms were very large. We negotiated the sale of the house and bought it on my GI Bill, with a small down payment, and low monthly payments. This was our first purchase of a home. The landscaping had not been completed, so I cut a deal with our agent. It was agreed that I would finish the landscaping for a substantial credit.

Oh, how I cursed myself many times for taking on that landscaping assignment. What a backbreaking job it turned out to be. Before I completed the work, I wished a thousand times that I had let the builder do the landscaping. As I discovered, I just didn't really have the time, with my regular job and my other responsibilities. But I did get it done, finally.

On April 13, 1956, a Friday, I was at work. I received a call from Mary Ann saying that she was ready to go to the hospital and have our second child. I dropped everything and left for home immediately. When I arrived, Mary Ann had everything packed and ready to go. I was so excited. I asked her if I would have time to take a quick shower, and she said I would. After finishing my shower, I got dressed, and called Jean Shoemaker, a friend of ours, if we could drop Edward off at her house, so that I could take Mary Ann to the hospital. She said that of course it would be fine. The Shoemakers had a little boy the same age as Edward.

As we were driving to the hospital, we discovered that I had on two different colors of socks. One was white, and the other was blue. I guess I had been really excited. Mary Ann had called ahead to inform Dr. Clayton that we were on our way to the hospital. We had only been there about 15 minutes, when

Dr. Clayton walked in. He had the nurse prepare Mary Ann for delivery. They asked that I wait in the waiting room with the rest of the fathers-to-be.

About forty-five minutes later, a nurse came into the waiting room and said that Dr. Clayton would like me to come to the delivery room. The nurse escorted me in. Dr. Clayton told us that it looked like the baby would not be arriving before tomorrow morning and that he and his wife had made arrangements with friends of theirs for an outing. He wanted to know if it would it be okay with us if he induced Mary Ann's labor. He assured us that she was in the best of health and that there wouldn't be any complications whatsoever. Mary Ann was tired of carrying this baby around. She was ready to be a mother, again. We both agreed that her labor should be induced and the delivery should proceed without delay. In those days they were very strict about not having the father in the delivery room during delivery. Mary Ann would rather not have had me in there anyway. So I went back to the waiting room with the rest of the expecting fathers

Mary Ann didn't seem to be at all nervous about having this baby, but I sure was. This would be my first time witnessing the ordeal of having a baby, especially my own. It seemed like I had been in that waiting room for ten hours before the baby was born. I remember drinking lots of coffee, and smoking lots of cigarettes. I remember calling Jean to inquire about Edward, and to let her know that the baby hadn't arrived yet. It was a very tense time for me. At about 8:15 that evening, a nurse came through the waiting room with a newborn baby wrapped in a surgical cloth.

"Mr. Herring?"

"Yes?"

She said, "This is your newborn little boy."

Wow, I was thrilled to death. I couldn't believe my own eyes. The baby hadn't even been cleaned up, yet. He had just arrived. He had the look of a baby that was saying, boy, am I glad to get out of there. He was really frowning. I will never forget that look he had on his little face. The nurse said that it was okay for me to go be with my wife, and as soon as she had the baby all cleaned up, she would bring him back into the room for us.

Dr. Clayton assured me that Mary Ann and baby were both doing fine and then both of us that Mary Ann would receive the best of care during her stay in the hospital. He told us that if anything out of the ordinary came up, the hospital staff knew how to reach him. If he were needed, he would return immediately. We thanked him, and bade him farewell.

I called Jean to inform her of the arrival of our new baby boy. She was so thrilled. I asked her if she would tell Edward about the arrival of his new baby brother. She said she would. I could sense that Mary Ann was getting a little drowsy, so I told her that I would leave and return tomorrow with Edward. She said okay, that was probably best. She told me to give Edward a hug and a kiss for her. I said I would. I knelt by the side of the bed, kissed her good-bye, and reminded her of how proud I was of her, and how happy I was with our new little baby boy.

When I arrived at Jean's house, Edward was fast asleep, so Jean, her husband Alvin and I chatted for a while. Alvin Shoemaker and I go back along ways. He and I were friends before either one of us got married. Alvin and I still remain the best of friends. Jean is no longer with Alvin; she passed away with cancer, on January 29, 2000.

It was getting pretty late, so I bid Alvin and Jean goodnight. I picked up Edward, and carried him out to the car.

As we were driving home, Edward woke up and said, in his cheerful little voice, "Oh, hi, Daddy. How are mommy and my little brother doing?"

I said they were doing fine. I told him that we had to go home and get a good night sleep, because tomorrow we would go to see them. He said, "Oh good," and was asleep before we got home. The next morning after breakfast, I gave Edward his bath, dressed him, and turned on the television so that he could watch cartoons, while I was taking my shower. On the way to Jefferson Hillman Hospital, Edward was very excited about the birth of his baby brother. He asked lots of questions: "Can

I play with him? Will he know who I am? What's his name?" The questions tumbled out of him. It took me a moment but I answered and told him that mommy and I hadn't decided on a name yet, but we would have one before the day was over. I also had to explain that he probably wouldn't be able to play with his brother just yet.

When we arrived at the hospital, we went directly to Mary Ann's room, and there, waiting for us, was mommy and baby brother. They were fresh and clean. Mary Ann had a big smile on her face and she asked Edward to come and give mommy a hug and a kiss.

Edward was thrilled. His first words were, "How are you feeling mommy?" Mary Ann assured him that she was fine. "Would you like to hold your little baby brother?" Edward's face lit up and he said, "Yes." As she handed Edward his little brother, she told him to be careful with his little head.

Sitting in that chair next to Mary Ann, Edward looked so cute holding his little baby brother. He started kissing him on his little cheeks. He was so excited. After the kissing and hugging was over, Mary Ann asked me if I had come up with a name for our baby. I asked her if she had come up with a name yet. We both laughed, and decided that we should name him after both our dads and our two brothers. Edward said that he was getting hungry, so Mary Ann told me to take him to the cafeteria right there in the hospital and get him a little lunch. We went back to Mommy's room, and Mommy was breast-feeding Arnold. Edward didn't know what to think.

He asked his mommy, "Why is baby brother biting you?" Mommy laughed and said, "He's not biting me. This is the way he has to be fed until he gets a little bigger." Edward said, "Oh! Did you feed me that way when I was a baby?" Mommy said, "Yes I did."

Edward began to get a little fidgety and just a little bored, so he asked me if he could go and play in the playroom. The hospital had a special playroom with toys, crayons, and coloring books. Mary Ann said that she was fine, and for me to take Edward into the playroom for a while. We were in there for about an hour, when Edward asked to go back and see Mommy and his baby brother. It was time to feed the baby again, and Edward, not for one moment, took his eyes off his mommy and baby brother. He was a very excited little boy. It was getting late, so Edward and I wished mommy and Arnold goodnight. As we were leaving Edward said to his Mommy," I love you mommy, and I love my baby brother too."

She said, "I love you too, and you be a good boy for daddy."

I kissed mommy and Arnold, and I told them we would see them both the next day.

On our way home, Edward kept asking questions about why Arnold had to be fed by sucking milk from Mommy's breast.

I knew the answer, but I said to him, "Let's wait until Mommy comes home. She will explain it to you much better than I can."

He said, "Okay."

Jean had invited Edward and I over for dinner that evening, so we stopped by and enjoyed dinner with them. She was a very good friend.

The next day, we went through the same procedure. Mommy and Arnold were doing fine. Edward got to watch mommy breast-feed Arnold, again. Mary Ann said that she was doing fine, and she wanted to go home. But the nurse said that she thought it would be best for her to wait until Dr. Clayton had checked her out. He would be returning to the hospital the next day, which was Monday. I had already made arrangements with the company to take off for a few days until Mary Ann was able to care for herself and the kids. In those days, management was very understanding regarding the needs of their employees and their families, particularly when newborns were involved. The next day, Dr. Clayton arrived at the hospital bright and early, even before Edward and I arrived. I didn't even get to talk to him. But Mary Ann said that he had checked her and Arnold out. He said that it would be okay for them to be released from the hospital in the afternoon.

When Edward and I arrived later in the day, Mary Ann was up and about, all dressed, and ready to go home. Arnold had a little cap on his head, and Mary Ann had dressed him in a pair of pajamas that her mother had sent to him. It wasn't check out time, but Mary Ann was ready to go home. The nurse said that it was okay for them to leave a little early. So, they put Mommy into a wheelchair, and escorted her out to the car. Edward walked along beside her, holding onto the wheelchair. I carried Arnold out in a bassinet that I had brought with me; it had been a baby gift from our friend Jean Shoemaker.

Dr. Clayton had been a very special physician throughout Mary Ann's pregnancy with Arnold. He was also the company doctor for the U.S. Pipe and Foundry Company. He would be at the job site at a specified time at each blast furnace location. This was so employees who had an ailment or a medical problem could have it looked at by the company doctor – on-site. It saved a lot of time-off from the job that way. He was a very special person in the eyes of the employees at U.S. Pipe. He always treated everyone with the utmost respect. We could always recognize from his demeanor the concern he had for all employees, black and white. He was very devoted to the medical profession and to the human race in general. I wished many times that he had been around when our family struggled and suffered with the greatest tragedy of our lives. [It was a tragedy that we would endure at a later time in our lives.]

The weather was a little chilly when we arrived at home. Mary Ann made sure that little Arnold was sufficiently wrapped in a warm blanket. I got out first and went to unlock the door of the house, and then went back to help Mary Ann and Arnold out. Edward was a great help. He carried mommy's little night bag in. He wanted to be helpful. I have always admired my son Edward. He was always anxious to do the right thing. He was such a blithe, remarkable child, and even until this day, he is a great person. I truly love him.

After putting everything in place, Mary Ann said, "It sure is nice to be home again." She told Edward that it was time for her to feed his baby brother again. And as she set in the rocking chair, rocking, and nursing Arnold. Edward, who as a little spectator was watching this spectacular event, found it all beyond comprehension for his little mind. I recall him asking mommy, how long will baby brother be eating that way?

Mommy said, "Oh, until he gets a little older and then he will be weaned." Edward said, "What does weaned mean?" Mommy said, "Well, it means that Arnold will gradually become accustomed to a bottle, that's filled with cow's milk, and the bottle will have a nipple on it, so that he can suck the milk out of the bottle, rather than Mommy having to breast feed him. You remember, don't you when you used to suck milk out of the bottle." I went out into the kitchen, and brought a bottle and nipple back to show him. He said, "Oh yes, I remember." He was satisfied and went on playing and watching.

Things were going well for us. I had a steady income, a new home, a wonderful wife and two beautiful little boys. What more could a man ask for in life?

Before long, Mary Ann and I thought that we should consider buying a second car. She needed transportation for grocery shopping, and going back and forth to the doctor when the kids had an ailment of some kind. So I bought a used car from one of the men on the job. He wanted to trade it in on a new car, but I convinced him to sell it to me for cash, and then he could use the cash as a down payment on his new car. The used car was really in good shape; I had learned a lot about used cars from my Army days. It was a 2 door, 1952 Chevrolet, coupe.

The neighborhood that we were living in was all right, but we grew tired of it, and decided to try and sell the house, in hopes of making a good profit. We called the agent that we had bought the house from originally, and gave her the listing. It hadn't been on the market for even a month, when one evening we received a call from our agent, saying that she had a prospect for our house, and she would like to show the house the next day, which was Saturday. We agreed on a time, and she said that it would be best if we would leave for a couple of hours, while she was showing the house. That was fine with us. We needed to do some shopping anyway.

When we returned home, about four hours later, there was a note lying on the kitchen table, from our agent. The note said for us to call her at home later on in the evening. When I called, she said, "They liked your house, and they have made an offer." I asked what the price was that they had offered. She said, "With him being a Veteran himself, they will pay you your equity plus 20%, and would assume your fixed rate VA loan." She went on to say that they wanted to move in on the day of closing. I told her that Mary Ann and I would talk it over, and that we would get back with her around the first of the week.

We both decided that their offer was a good one, so, we agreed to accept it. However, I remember Mary Ann saying that we would have to get busy, trying to find us a place to rent. The next day was Sunday, and we looked in the paper for a house to rent. Sure enough, there was a two-bedroom house, not far from where we were living. I called the owner to make an appointment to see the house that day.

The house was located in Center Point, which was a little community not very far away. The house was situated in the middle of five acres, just off of the main highway into the city of Birmingham. About two acres in front, and about an acre in the back of the house had already been cultivated. The other two acres had nice big tall pine trees. It was a beautiful place.

The owner seemed to like us, so his price for rental was only $150 a month with the first and last month rent in advance. However, he said that he would waive the first and last months payment, and reduce the monthly payment to $75, providing I cut the grass on a twice a week basis. Of course we accepted his terms, and informed him that we wouldn't be able to move in for another three weeks or so. He told us that would not be a problem. He stuck out his hand for a handshake, and said we had a deal, and no paper work would be necessary. This guy was something else.

That evening, I called our agent to inform her that we had decided to accept her clients' offer on our house. She said that she would notify them immediately. She also stated that her clients were pre-qualified, and that she would expect the sale to close sooner than expected. I said that would be fine with us, because we wanted to move as soon as possible.

Within the next two weeks our agent notified us that everything was a go, and that we could start moving out anytime. So, I called our new landlord to inform him that we would like to start moving in. He said, "That's wonderful." He asked whether we needed any help moving our furniture. "No thanks; you're doing enough as it is." Mary Ann started packing things into boxes and I borrowed a flatbed truck from a friend of mine to move our furniture. As a matter of fact, this friend of mine helped me with the loading and unloading of our furniture. His name was Leon Alford. Leon, whom we all called Doc, was a good person and a friend to all. Unfortunately, Doc was a heavy smoker, and consumed lots of alcohol. Four years later, Doc had a massive heart attack and died, leaving behind his wife and two small girls. He was greatly missed by all.

About three months after settling into our new home, Mary Ann said that she would like to take a trip to Seattle to visit her family. She was anxious for her mother and the rest of the family to see our new baby boy. So, we called the train station and made reservations. Her only change of trains would be in Chicago. She was able to get a sleeper, so that she and the kids would be able to sleep in comfort at night. The trip to Seattle would take about two and a half days. I wasn't able to take any more time off from work or I would have gone with them. I sure missed them while they were away. Luckily for me, while they were gone, I was occupied with lots of overtime, due to fact that one of the boilers needed a complete overhaul. That kept me busy, plus cutting three acres of grass twice a week.

When Mary Ann and the boys arrived in Seattle, Bill and Helen were there to meet them. She called me to inform me that they had arrived safely. As it turned out, Mary Ann's oldest sister, Bernice, was also there to visit. It was a good reunion for them. Bernice had a little boy by the name of Tommy Harman. He was six months older than Arnold.

Mary Ann called me on a Saturday night, and I wasn't at home to receive her call. She later said, "My brother Bill said that you were probably out running around with another woman." Bill said that was what all men did when their wives were away from home. I could tell that she was upset over the statement that her brother had made, so I assured her that his statement was not true. When she called, I was at our friends' house, Alvin and Jean Shoemaker's. They had invited me over for dinner and I had taken them up on their offer. Bill later told Mary Ann that he was only kidding her. He always did like to kid his little sister.

When Mary Ann was ready to leave Seattle, she called me to let me know when they would be arriving in Birmingham. I was there to meet them, and never was I so glad to see anyone in my entire life. They were so glad to see me, too. I remember Edward saying, "Daddy, I sure did miss you. Did you miss us? I said, "I sure did." Mary Ann, ever the practical one, said that they were starving to death. They hadn't had a bite to eat since lunch. So we stopped at a nearby restaurant for dinner. It was great to be all together again.

Edward also asked how his little puppy was doing. Before Mary Ann and the kids went to Seattle, Edward had said that he would like to have a puppy for a little pet. So, we read in the paper where this lady had a litter of Collie pups for sale. We called her for directions to her place. Edward picked out the puppy that he thought was the prettiest and we paid the lady $25 for it and left for home. Edward was really happy to have a little pet. It was a very pretty little female pup. However, the puppy had taken sick before they had left on their trip to Seattle. While they were away, I took the puppy to a veterinarian. He diagnosed the puppy with Hepatitis, an inflammation of the liver. He advised me to have the puppy put to sleep, which I did. I sure did hate to tell Edward about the loss of his puppy. But I did, and he understood. I assured him that I would get him another puppy later on.

Mr. Bailey, who was our landlord, also owned and lived on a ten-acre parcel adjacent to the five acres that we were renting. He had some cows corralled in a section of his place, and said that if I wanted to buy a baby calf to raise, that it would be okay to raise it in his corral. Later he extended an offer for us to buy the five acres that we were renting for $11,000. At that time $11,000 was all the money in the world. I thanked him, but we declined his generous offer. I just wasn't into buying farm land at the time. (This, of course, remains one of my regrets in life). Several years later, Mary Ann and I went back to visit with my folks in Birmingham. While we were there we drove out to Center Point where the five acres had been. We discovered that Mr. Bailey had sold the five-acre parcel to a chain, and they built a shopping center. He was paid one million bucks for it. What a missed opportunity!

After a little while, we decided to move again and rented a house on 7th Avenue North, in East Lake. This is where we were living when a neighbor's dog had a litter of Collie pups and she gave us one for Edward. We named the pup, Dixie. She was a female. We only lived in this house for a few months before we went house shopping to buy a house that would be near the school that Edward and Arnold would soon be attending. It was the Robinson Elementary School in East Lake. We found a nice 3-bedroom home at 8504 3rd Avenue North. This house would really serve our needs. It had a nice fenced back yard, which was ideal for Dixie, Edward's dog. The total price for the house was $11,500. We bought it through FHA, with a 25% down payment. Our family would reside there on 3rd Avenue for the next seven years.

Mary Ann started buying furniture for our house. I must say that her choices were very expensive. They were all Ethan Allen. But I must say that she made the right choices. Even to this day, we still have all the furniture that Mary Ann purchased during that time. We also became active in community affairs, such as church, Sunday school, Civitan Club, Masonic Lodge. I taught Sunday school and was a little league baseball coach for three years.

During this period I had the opportunity to attend school at the University Center of Alabama. I also took classes at Birmingham Business College, for higher accounting. I received a certificate from The Raymond J. Horn, School of

Drafting, and a certificate from Jefferson County Public School in Blueprint Reading. I also attended school at Jefferson County Vocational School in welding. (All the classes were at night). I was a very ambitious young man. My goal was to obtain, and absorb all the education that I possibly could. To me, the value of an education cannot be over emphasized. Throughout my life I have encouraged, and supported, young people in their efforts to obtain an education. Some have accepted my advice, and some have not accepted my advice. I must say, some of the ones that have accepted my advice, turned out to be very successful in business. I am happy for them and their families.

Edward and Arnold were very happy little boys. They played together very well. Edward was very protective of his little brother. I can't recall any incidents of Edward and Arnold fighting with one another. Both were delightful and cheerful little boys. However, Arnold was a very inquisitive child. Whenever he got a toy, no matter what kind, he would dismantle it to find out what made it tick. He would then put it back together. And, of course, he was always into things, just like Edward was. But, his curiosity got him into any number of problems.

One evening, Arnold opened the doors of our laundry room, where we kept the detergents, such as bleach, washing power. He swallowed some bleach, and became very sick. I called the emergency room at the hospital, and luckily Dr. Clayton was on call. When we arrived, he was waiting for us. They put Arnold on a gurney, and wheeled him into the operating room. Mary Ann and I stayed with him. In the operating room, Dr. Clayton asked that I hold him down while he inserted the suction tube down his throat to suck out the fluids. Arnold was having his stomach pumped. I will never forget Arnold looking up at me with tears in his little eyes. He was asking me, with his eyes, "What is Dr. Clayton doing to him?" When he had finished with Arnold, Dr. Clayton wrote a prescription for us to get filled. He said to give him a teaspoon full of this liquid every four hours, until he got to feeling better. He assured us that he would be okay.

Another time Arnold was injured when he was running through the hallway of the house, buck naked and tripped over a toy lying in the middle of the hall. He landed on the floor furnace grate, which was very hot, and fried his little butt. We didn't take him to the doctor for that incident. Mary Ann just rubbed some salve over his butt and he had to walk around for a few days without any diapers on. It healed up pretty fast, but it was very uncomfortable for him. (However, the worst incident is still to come).

Arnold's baby teeth were just coming in, when again, as he was running through the living room he tripped, and fell on the corner of an end table, landing on his mouth. The impact drove his two little front teeth up into his gums. It was a terrible sight to see all this blood pouring out of our little boy's mouth. Mary Ann called our dentist, and he said to bring him over as soon as possible. We grabbed both of the kids, and rushed over to his office.

When we arrived, the dentist was waiting for us. There was another lady ahead of us, but knowing the circumstances, she said that she would come back another time. Mary Ann was holding Arnold in her arms, with a towel covering his little mouth. He was bleeding profusely, and sobbing at the same time. The dentist asked that I hold Arnold while he administered a shot of Novocain. This was a very difficult task for me. As it turned out, the dentist had to administer two shots of Novocain. The first shot hurt, and Arnold screamed at the top of his lungs. He managed to ask me for help! I tried to soothe him down as much I possibly could. There was nothing that I could do to comfort my little boy. The dentist removed both of his front baby teeth. It took several years for his permanent teeth to grow in and when they did start to grow, they came in twisted. This was because his other baby teeth were growing into the space where his two front baby teeth had been. Needless to say, he had to wear braces throughout his teen-age years. It was a very long and expensive time for him and for us. Even today, I think he may still have some problems with his teeth.

Dixie, the Collie pup, grew into a beautiful dog. She was very playful with the kids. They loved her dearly. Our only problem was that she didn't appreciate being cooped up in the back yard. Consequently, she would display her frustration by barking, and I mean barking loudly. The neighbors complained quite a bit. She would run around and around in the back yard. Before long, she had cut a trail with her running. She kept us busy trying to keep her calmed down. She remained this way up until she came into heat. A friend of ours had a male Collie, and he agreed to let his Collie hook up with Dixie, providing that he got first choice of the litter. So it was a done deal. He brought his male over, and left him over night to mate with Dixie. I watched the event as it took place. I thought they stayed hooked up longer than what they should. But, then I somehow had gotten a little prudish along the way. I guess children have that effect on parents. Eventually they separated, and remained cool and calm the rest of the night. Since then, I have learned more about why they could not separate right away.

Dixie never barked any more after she became pregnant. When it was time for her to whelp, we prepared a nice, warm place for her on the back porch. It was enclosed. On the evening of her giving birth to her puppies, the temperature was about 10 above. It was a very cold night in January. However, during the early hours of the morning she whelped 13 of the cutest puppies we had ever seen. She only had enough room for 12 of them to nurse. So, Mary Ann used one of the kid's bottles and a nipple, and nursed the runt of the litter throughout the entire ordeal. They all grew into a healthy bunch of pups. It was quite a spectacular view watching them follow behind Dixie as she walked around the path that she had created. When they came of age, we gave the pick of the litter to our friend with the father of the pups and then put the remaining 11 up for sale. They sold very rapidly.

After Edward and Arnold started school, Mary Ann was offered a job with the Plumbers and Pipe Fitters Union, to serve as a Secretary for the Joint Apprenticeship Committee. My little sister, Letha would come over to our house, and stay with the boys until Mary Ann arrived. It was a very nice job for Mary Ann. She enjoyed it tremendously. The people that she worked with were very vigorously Democrats, and great supporters of George Wallace, who was campaigning for the Governor of Alabama. A landslide eventually elected him to his first term.

I continued working at US Pipe. At the time I didn't realize that this would be where I would acquire the greatest experience of my lifetime. I had attended and served an apprenticeship with the Ironworkers Union # 92 in Birmingham, but the training that I received there was nothing compared to the training that I received at US Pipe. I was privileged to have served and worked with some of the finest people on earth, from management on down. Acknowledgements of these wonderful people will be in the back of this book.

During most of my employment with US Pipe, I worked at #3 and #4 Blast Furnaces, which were located in North Birmingham. I was working there during the construction of a new Blast Furnace #5. Rust Engineering Company of Birmingham was the General Contractor for the construction of this furnace. After the construction had been completed on # 5, most of us were transferred to other furnaces. My last year with US Pipe, I worked at #1 and #2 on First Avenue.

We received a letter from Kathy, (Mary Ann's niece in Seattle). She invited us to come to Seattle, to attend the Worlds Fair. We gladly accepted her invitation, and the both of us put in for our vacation time. It was the consensus of our employers that it would be okay to take our vacations at the time we had requested. We began to prepare for the trip that lay ahead of us. We were really excited about going to a Worlds Fair. Before leaving for Seattle, I had purchased four new Goodyear tires for our new 4-door-1958 Oldsmobile. We planed to drive west, instead of flying, because we had always enjoyed the scenery going and coming from Seattle. In those days, I could and did drive to Seattle and back for only $70 each way. Except for the time spent on the road, it was a lot cheaper to drive than fly. Motels and food were fairly cheap in those days as well.

On the day before we were to depart for Seattle, my

Foreman, Mike Gamble, said that he had some bad news for me. He told me that the boss George Miller, the Superintendent at Blast Furnace # 1 and 2. He decided that I would not be able to take my vacation for at least another three weeks. Even though I rightly had two weeks of vacation time coming and had scheduled it with the company well in advance of our departure. What to do!?

I knew that Mary Ann and the kids would be terribly disappointed if we were to cancel our trip. We were already packed and ready to go. I said to Mike, "Well Mike, you can tell George that I am sorry, but I will be taking my two weeks of vacation starting Monday morning." Mike said that he understood, but that he was only doing his job.

That evening, when Mary Ann and I sat down for dinner at home, she was shocked when I informed her of my situation. She asked me what I was going to do. I said, "What do you think I am going to do? As soon as we drop Letha off at my parent's house, we will be leaving for Seattle, job or no job." She said, "Good." I could see worry lines beside her smile.

We drove the biggest part of the night. I wanted to get as far as I possibly could before having to stop to sleep. During the first part of our journey, we discussed the consequences of our return trip back home. Mary Ann asked the question, "Do you think they will fire you when we return home?" I remember answering with something like, "Oh well, I think I did what any young American would do under the circumstances. George had no right whatsoever to deny me my vacation on the day before we were to leave. Whatever the consequences may be, I will have to accept them." We drove practically all day and all night. However, we did stop occasionally at a motel, but only when we felt like we needed to rest. We also ate very well on this trip. Edward and Arnold were very sound sleepers. And they were always able to entertain themselves and play quietly. They were a pleasure to travel with.

On the following Monday morning at 10 a.m. (Seattle time), we pulled up in front of Helen's apartment. No one was there at the time of our arrival, but Mary Ann had a key to the apartment, so we let ourselves in. Helen was at work, and when she got home, she was surprised to see us there so soon. We had called her before leaving Birmingham, to let her know that we were leaving for Seattle that Friday evening. She didn't expect us to arrive until the following Wednesday.

We slept for most of that first day in Seattle. That evening, Helen told us that Margaret had invited us over for dinner. So we left to have dinner with Mary Ann's sister and her family. Helen had already purchased our tickets for the Seattle World's Fair, so we wouldn't have to stand in line to buy tickets. Believe me, there was a crowd of people standing in line to buy tickets the next day. When we parked in the parking lot near the Space Needle, there were cars with out-of-state tags on them from all over the United States. We visited the Fair on three consecutive days. We thoroughly enjoyed the spectacular colors, the international pavilions, the exhibits and the interesting events of the Fair. We were able to eat lunch at the top of the Space Needle every day. From the top of the revolving Space Needle, we had a view of the fairgrounds and beautiful buildings below. The wondrous and fascinating panorama of the Olympic Mountains, Puget Sound, its shipping and islands, the Cascade Mountains capped by Mt. Rainier to the East and Mt. Baker to the North and the city of Seattle surrounded by this beauty, was what convinced me to return to Seattle to live.

The rest of our vacation was spent with Mary Ann's family. The following Sunday, we all packed a picnic lunch and met at Cottage Lake in Woodinville. At that time, property was selling dirt cheap in Woodinville. Our vacation was drawing to a close, so we packed the car, and kissed and hugged everyone good-bye, and away we went. During our journey back to Birmingham, Mary Ann and I talked about what we might find when I showed back up for work on Monday morning. Whatever happened, I was prepared for the worst.

We left Seattle a couple of days sooner than I normally would have, but we did so to give ourselves a couple of extra days of rest before the kids would have to be back in school and before. Mary Ann would report back to work.

Monday morning, I reported back to work, clocked in, and was going about my usual business, when Mike Gamble approached me and said that George wanted to see me in his office. When I arrived at his office, he was very calm, cool, and collected, but so was I. I was prepared for the worst, and sure enough, the worst did come.

He said, "I am going to let you go, because you disregarded my orders not to take your vacation when you did." He handed me my two weeks vacation paycheck that was due me. All I said to him was, happy memories, and left his office. I could have protested, but I didn't. Actually, I felt kind of relieved. I knew that there were other challenges out there for me, somewhere, maybe even Seattle.

I went out to the blast furnace to bid farewell to all of my friends, that I had shared so many good times with during the last seven 7 years. This was what I would miss most, working with such good men. I left the grounds of US Pipe and immediately went to the bank to deposit my check. Next I went to the Ironworkers Union Hall to check in to see if they had any work listed that I might apply for. Charlie Green, the Business Agent for the Ironworkers Union, and I had become pretty good friends over the years. He and Mary Ann had also become acquainted through their work with the Unions. Mary Ann represented the Pipe Fitters Union, and Charlie represented the Ironworkers Union. So there was a certain amount of politics involved between the Unions, and I must say that it helped to have some inside pull.

Charlie said that American Bridge Company had placed a call for a welder at the TCI (Tennessee Coal Iron) plant in Fairfield, which was just on the outskirts of Birmingham. He said if I wanted the job, it was mine. However, he said, "You'll have to work the evening shift from 3-11 PM." I told him that would be fine with me, but only until a day shift job came open. He agreed and after only three hours of unemployment, I was back in the workforce. I called Mary Ann at her office and informed her about what had taken place at US Pipe, and she told me that she wasn't surprised. Then I told her about my new job and said I was going straight there. I said I'd be home around midnight.

I had been working at American Bridge for about three months when one morning, the phone rang it was Charlie Green on the other end. He said, "Charlie, how would you like to go to work for a Texas Company as a foreman? (He also called me Charlie). I said, "Sure, why not?" He then explained to me what the job was all about. Fransworth and Chambers out of Houston, Texas had called him to say that they had received a contract to build a seven-story nurses' home in Birmingham. They said they would need an Ironworker Foreman. Charlie told me that they would be breaking ground in about three weeks. Fransworth said that they would like to have the Ironworker Foreman to be on site, during the excavation. This would be a guaranteed 40 hours per week job. I thanked Charlie for this opportunity. This would be my first management assignment.

About a week later, Charlie called to tell me that he had submitted my name and phone number to The Company, and that I could expect a call from their Superintendent, Tag Almond, within a week or so. Sure enough, the following Thursday, I received a call from Tag to find out how soon I would be able to start to work. I told him that I would like to give my present employer notice before quitting. Tag said that he could understand that and for me to call him as soon as I knew when I could begin my new job. He left his phone number with me. The next day I informed Blackie Thacker, who was the general foreman for American Bridge that I would be quitting, because I had been offered another job as a foreman. During my earlier years with American Bridge in Houston, Texas, and New Orleans, Blackie had been my Foreman on both jobs. He said, "Chuck, I wish you all the luck in the world, and if you ever need a job, be sure and call me." He stated that he had recognized my potential and my ability to become a Foreman, or even a Superintendent. That really made me feel good.

I placed a call to Tag to tell him that I would be available for work on Monday.

He said, "Great," I'll see you on the job site around 10 Monday morning"

When I arrived at the job site, Tag was helping the driver park his job trailer. Greetings were in order.

After they parked the trailer, Tag said, "Let's go over to the coffee shop and have a cup of coffee."

While sipping on our coffee, we exchanged backgrounds and became pretty well acquainted. Tag had a degree in Construction Management from Texas A&M, and had been employed with Fransworth & Chambers for the past three years. This was the only Construction Company he had worked for since graduating from college. He started out with them as an Assistant Superintendent. On the completion of his first job, he was promoted to Superintendent.

He explained what my responsibilities would be, as his Foreman, on this job. He must have really taken a liking to me, because before we left the coffee shop he said that, instead of you being just a foreman, he would like me to assume the responsibility of serving as their Ironworker Superintendent for the Birmingham area. He told me that Fransworth & Chambers was planning on more work in the Birmingham area. Since I had been highly recommended by Charlie Green, at the Union, Tag felt that I had the right qualifications for this job. I was really flattered since I had never supervised a construction job in my entire life.

This was a lucky break for me.

It didn't take very long for the truck driver to set up the job trailer, which was 12-ft. X 60 ft. It had four partitioned rooms to serve as office spaces, and a restroom. Tag's office was, of course, the largest and was located near the front of the trailer. My office was in the middle of the trailer and was only large enough for a desk, chair, filing cabinet, a drawing board, and a plan holder. I was really impressed, "Wow!" I was management with a title and an office. Maybe going on vacation when I was told not to had been the right move after all.

I had plenty of time to become familiar with the blueprints, elevations, and the orientation of the building. In the meantime,

Tag hired Dan O'Neal, a Civil Engineer just out of College. This would be Dan's first job. The Carpenter Superintendent's real name was never known to any of us, we just called him "Bruno." He had worked for the Company in Texas for the past five years, and had been transferred to Birmingham just to do this job. Tag also hired a local young lady as a secretary. She shared the office space with Tag.

My responsibilities were to hire a foreman, and a crew to place the reinforcing steel, and to install all miscellaneous steel, and to erect all structural steel. Hiring a good crew wasn't a hard task because Charlie Green, (Ironworkers Business Agent) had already selected a crew of good men for this job. One of them would be my Dad. I would also coordinate all steel deliveries from the local vendors. Ceco Steel was the vendor that would supply all of the reinforcing steel, completely detailed and fabricated. American Bridge would furnish all miscellaneous and structural steel, completely detailed and fabricated.

When the excavation of the footings was completed, we were ready to start placing the reinforcing steel. I had already placed an order into Ceco Steel for all of the footing steel, and had received the shipment the week before we were ready to install it. I called Charlie Green to request two Ironworkers to place the footing steel. One of the workers was my Dad, who would serve as the foreman on the job. The other Ironworker was Howard Champion. Howard and Dad were good friends.

The job and the experience were very good for me. I gained a lot of knowledge in management and supervision during the thirteen months that I was employed with Fransworth & Chambers. When the job was nearing completion, Tag said that if I wanted too, I could relocate to Houston, and work in that area for the Company. They had plenty of work there. He said the Company would pay for all our moving expenses, etc. But I declined his generous offer. We were not ready to move to Texas.

Fransworth & Chambers, through their bidding procedures had run into some difficulties, better known in the construction world as "competition." Their competitors weren't about to allow a Texas outfit to underbid them in Birmingham. This seven-story nurse's home had been a negotiated job. In other words, they didn't have to bid on this job. So, Fransworth & Chambers pulled up stakes and went back to Houston, Texas.

Our house needed painting; so, I took two weeks off, and painted the house. It also needed a new roof; so, I put a new roof on it as well. After I had finished with my honey-do list, I received a call from Charlie Green, saying that Guy F. James Construction Company had a call in for a crew of Rod-men on the Logan Martin Dam, in Pell City, Alabama, and wanted to know if I were interested. By now, I was interested in working again. "You bet!" He asked me if I thought Willie (my Dad) would be interested, too? I said that I didn't know, but for him to give Dad a call. He did call Dad, and we both accepted the job.

My Dad, and Howard Champion lived in Fairfield Highlands, which is on the outskirts of Birmingham. They would drive over to my house in East Lake every morning, leave their cars parked at our house, and the three of us would commute to the job in my new 1962-1/2 ton Chevy. Pick-up. When we arrived on the job site, it was like old homecoming week, we knew all of the Rod-men on the job.

A Rodman is a person that is skilled in the placing of Reinforcing Steel. After the Reinforcing Steel is placed in the proper wood forms, concrete is poured over it, which is known as poured-in-place concrete. A Structural Ironworker is a person that erects Structural Steel. Both are affiliated with the same Ironworkers Union. Depending on the experience of an individual, he may accept a job doing either trade, when called upon.

During the course of working on this job, I was fortunate to have met a Carpenter Foreman by the name of Bob Allen. Bob's duration on this job was to be very short. But during his stay, we became pretty good friends. His lifetime experience had been nothing but working on dams throughout the United States. He was waiting to be called to a job in Colorado. His very close friend, who was the General Superintendent, was scheduled to call him as soon as the job required his services.

One morning, Bob approached me and said, "Well Charlie, I am dragging up, last night I received the call that I have been waiting for from Colorado. They want me to be there within a week." ("Dragging up" means "quitting") Bob said, "They will also be needing a General Foreman for the placement of all of the Reinforcing Steel on this project. Would I be interested in that job?"

I said, "I don't know, I would have to check with my wife. He said, "OK, let me know tomorrow, because it will be my last day." Driving home after work that evening, I told my Dad and Howard about the offer that Bob had presented to me. They both encouraged me to take the offer. However, my Dad was a little more reluctant than Howard was.

Dad said," It will be very hard on your Mom and Sisters; they would miss you a ton, especially the boys, Edward and Arnold." But, Dad knew that eventually I would branch out, seeking my own goals in life. At home that evening, Edward and Arnold ran out to the truck, and hugged and kissed their Grandpa. They were always happy to see him. Dad and Howard drove away. Mary Ann and I talked about the Colorado offer I had received. I recall Mary Ann saying that she had always wanted to go to Colorado, but she wasn't sure about living there. She remembered as a kid, when she lived in Humphrey, Nebraska, and all the snow. She particularly remembered walking to school through drifts of snow nearly as high as she was. But she would be willing to do whatever I decided to do.

The next day, I informed Bob that I would accept the offer. I told him that I was curious as to just when this offer would come about. Before we made the move, Mary Ann would have to quit her job, and take the boys out of school. He said, "I can assure you that you will have plenty of time." Mary Ann and I continued to work on our jobs, while waiting for the call about Colorado. We had just about given up on them ever calling me. I remember telling Mary Ann that I thought Bob had been pulling my leg.

But, on the following Sunday evening, the phone rang, and a voice said, "Hi, Charlie, this is Van Graham in Colorado.

I am the General Superintendent for Tecon Corporation, of Dallas, Texas." He went on to say that Tecon was the General Contractor that had been selected by the Bureau of Reclamation, to construct the Blue Mesa Dam in Sapinero, Colorado.

"Bob Allen has recommended you for the General Foreman's job to oversee the placement of the Reinforcing Steel here on this project. Are you were interested?"

My jaw nearly hit the floor but I answered, "Yes, I was very interested in the job."

He went on to tell me how much my salary would be. He also wanted to know when I thought I could report to the job. During our conversation, Van said that he and all of the other people on his staff were living in Gunnison, which is approximately 25 miles east of Sapinero. His family and most of the others were living in a trailer court. He told me that I would be guaranteed a salary of $195.00 per week. My salary would start as soon as I accepted the job offer. This amount of money was great at the time. The job was based upon 40 hours per week. He asked me to talk the proposition over with my wife and call him back (collect) the next day.

The minute I hung up the phone, Mary Ann and I started discussing this offer. We both realized that if I decided to accept their offer, I would have to leave her and the boys in Birmingham until I got situated in Colorado. It was a huge decision to make. As it was about time for dinner, we decided to take the boys out to the pancake house for Mickey Mouse Waffles. My motto has always been. "Do Not Make Critical Decisions on An Empty Stomach!"

When we returned to the house, it was time for the boys to go to bed. Once they were settled for the night, Mary Ann and I began examining the pros and cons of this move to Colorado. Mary Ann knew that I was seriously hoping she would push me out the door.

She said, "Honey, I think this could be your big opportunity. You are young, bright, and very ambitious; and always remember one thing; you can't steal second base with your foot on first." {I have always tried to remember her words]

She said for me not to worry about her and the kids. Edward was in the fourth grade, and Arnold was in the first grade. They would be fine, she said. She would notify the school about taking them out and she would submit her resignation to her employer.

Needless to say, this decision was a very exciting move for me. It was now time for me to put all of my schooling, and experience out ahead of me, and to get on with life. The next morning we got the boys off to school and Mary Ann journeyed off to her job. I placed a call to my employer, to inform them of our decision to leave for the Colorado job. My boss wished me good luck. I didn't even go to work that day. I asked that my paycheck be sent by mail.

I placed a collect call to Van Graham, informing him of our decision. He was glad that I had accepted his offer. I told him that I would be leaving for Colorado on Monday morning. He asked that I drive carefully over the mountains in Colorado, because the mountains and roads were full of snow. The temperature was 10 below zero. I assured him that I would be careful.

I spent the rest of the day packing the clothes that I would need, and having my truck serviced. I called Mary Ann to let her know that I had called Van informing him of our decision. She said, "Good." But, in my mind's ear, I could the worry in her voice.

I told her that I would meet her for lunch at the restaurant where the people at her office usually ate. This was a restaurant where all the Union Officials met and had lunch. It just so happened that my friend Charlie Green was there. I told him of my decision, and he too wished me the very best of luck. Charlie reminded me that if things didn't work out for me in Colorado I could always come back to Birmingham and find work.

On Sunday my Mother invited us over for lunch after church

The Civil Rights movement had already begun. Martin

Luther King had demonstrated his leadership among his followers stating," I have a dream... we shall overcome." Bull Conner, who was at the time the Police Chief of Birmingham, had already released the dogs on the demonstrators, who were only trying to achieve what they were entitled to in life, the freedom and opportunity to live and work, to receive the respect due any human being on the face of the earth. During my employment at US Pipe, there were many good black people who worked there. Even though we were all segregated (they were compelled to have their own private showers, toilets, drinking fountains, etc.) I was unaware of any discontent at all.

During my combat time in Korea, white and black soldiers had fought side by side. We all used the same showers; we ate in the same mess halls. We all thought that we were fighting for a great cause. I had never thought much about segregation issues as I had been born into them. They just seemed part of normal life. But when I returned from Korea, I became aware of the rot of prejudice and how it demeaned so many decent people. A black skin was no guaranty of evil. I knew and read about whites, for example, who slaughtered the Native Americans wholesale. Evil comes from the hearts of men, not their skins.

One thing that I can truly say is that my parents never taught us to hate another person, black or white. The schools that I attended never overtly displayed any racism that I can remember, or recognized at the time. I saw and heard individuals who acted and spoke out their racist ideas on school grounds, in the workplace, in KKK rallies on television. I read about the Nazis in Germany and their racist hatreds. I could not then nor can I now understand these hateful behaviors here in our own country or elsewhere.

The next morning, November 1, 1962, I got up very early. I don't think I even slept any during the night. I had everything packed and ready to go from the night before. I went into the kitchen and put the coffee on. Mary Ann must have smelled the hot brewing coffee, because she got out of bed to see me off. While we were sitting at the kitchen table sipping our coffee, she cautioned me to drive carefully, and to call her when I arrived in Colorado. I assured her that I would. A few minutes later, Edward and Arnold got out of bed, and came into the kitchen to hug and kiss me good-bye. I hated leaving them behind, but the decision had already been made, with no regrets.

Chapter 7

COLORADO

Mary Ann and I embraced and kissed, showing our passionate love for one another. Mary Ann's kisses always caused me to become eagerly aroused. The warmth of her body next to mine is pleasure beyond comprehension. I had to get on the road. All the way out to the truck, I could hear those little voices yelling at me, "Bye, bye Daddy, I love you."

As I journeyed off into the wild blue yonder, I felt sad but confident in the knowledge that the decision we had made would be for the best for my family, in the long run. I drove straight through, only stopping long enough to get gas, and a bite to eat, and to stretch my legs. While driving through Colorado, the snow-capped mountains reminded me of the mountains in Korea. There were times during my travel, as I looked to the far horizon of the snow capped Colorado mountains, I could see my fellow comrades struggling through the deep, cold, white snow in Korea. Once again I visited the sadness buried in my memories of seeing the blood soaked bodies that we had to carry through the snow. It was a chilling, but vivid memory. As I traveled forward, the disturbing memories gradually vanished from my mind, and were replaced with the sight of the beautiful sunset over the mountains of Colorado.

The town of Gunnison is located in the west central part of the state. It is approximately 250 miles west of Denver. Gunnison is the area of the Rockies that experiences the greatest snowfalls, some 38-ft. or more per year. The days are generally sunny. It has been estimated that in Denver the sun shines an average of 67 per cent of the time between official sunrise and sunset. (Of course it would be hard for the sun to shine, even if there were no clouds, after sunset?) Institutions of higher education in the state include the Western State College of Colorado, at Gunnison. The state also maintains a school for the deaf and blind at Colorado Springs. Colorado has seventeen-state-run schools.

I arrived in Gunnison about 3 p.m. the following day. It had begun to snow. I sure was glad that I took Mary Ann's advice about bringing my heavy winter coat with me. Man, it was cold! I pulled into town and stopped the truck in front of a small western cafe on the main street. There weren't very many people in the cafe at this time in the afternoon, so, I ordered a cup of coffee, and became aquatinted with a waiter, whose name was George Mason. George told me he was born and raised in Colorado Springs and had only lived in Gunnison for the past two weeks. He was a concrete laborer by trade, and was waiting for a call from the Union Hall to dispatch him out to the Blue Mesa Dam. They were to call him he said, when they were ready to start pouring concrete. But, in the meantime, he needed some income while he was waiting, so, he got paid for being a waiter.

I asked George if he knew where I could rent a room until I found a house for the family.

He told me that there was a boarding house about three blocks from the cafe and he was certain that there was a spare room available. He called the boarding house to verify his report, and yes, he found, they had a vacancy. He told the lady my name and that I would be by shortly and move in.

The boarding house was a quaint old western farmhouse that I found to be very clean. The landlady asked me where I was from, and I told her I was moving from Alabama. She said that was good, because she didn't like the people in town from Texas. I was lucky to have met George, and to have gotten the room when I did, because lots of construction workers were beginning to move in, getting ready to start work on the dam. The room cost $15 per week, payable in advance, no meals, just a room and bath and the bath had to be shared. After settling in, I took a stroll along the streets of Gunnison, and when I found a phone booth, I called Mary Ann to let her know that I had arrived safely.

She was happy to hear that I had made the trip safely, and she immediately began asking questions about the town of Gunnison. She had been reading up on the history of Gunnison. She said that she and the kids couldn't wait until they were with me. I assured her that as soon as I got settled in with my job that I would be coming back to get them. We must have talked for at least an hour before hanging up. It was a dysphoric (always wanted to use that word, "unhappy") time for me. I had only been away from them a few days, and it felt like I had been away for a month.

I finished talking with Mary Ann on the phone, went back into the cafe, and ordered a Chicken Fried Steak, with gravy and mashed potatoes. George was my waiter. He asked if I had gotten settled in, and I told him I had and thanked him for his help. After finishing with my dinner, he and I chatted for a while. I then left and went back to my room. I was pretty exhausted from the trip. I really slept that first night in Gunnison.

The next morning, I stopped by the cafe, had a cup of coffee and my thermos bottle filled with coffee. Then I drove out to the job site. When I arrived at the job site, a man strolled out towards my truck. He stuck out his hand and said, "You must be Charlie Herring?" I confirmed that I was. "I'm Van Graham. Nice to meet you." We shook hands. "I figured that it was you when I saw the license plates on your truck were from Alabama."

Van and I hit it off from the start. He took me by the carpenter's hangout where I found Bob Allen, who was responsible for my being in Colorado. It was good to see Bob again. Van then took me into the main office of Tecon, and introduced me to all of the staff. Payroll department was the first stop. I got signed up and they presented me with my first check. It's nice to get paid the day you report for work.

All of the Tecon staff seemed to be a great bunch of people. Most of them had worked on other projects like this one before. They were like a family that travels from one job to another.

After completing my orientation, Van took me out to the diversion tunnels that had to be lined with reinforcing steel, and poured with concrete. That would be my first job. The crew that was drilling through the hard rock of the mountain for the tunnels wasn't quite ready for the other crews to come in and start their work, yet. The carpenters, labors, and ironworkers would have to wait until the tunnels were drilled in the mountain before they could begin.

My first assignment was to work in the engineering department, familiarizing myself with the blueprints, schedules, and the sequence of operation. I also established contact with the steel fabricators, who were fabricating the reinforcing steel for this project. They were located in Dallas, Texas. I talked to their shop foreman and their transportation foreman and agreed on the sequence of deliveries for the steel.

I had called Mary Ann several times from my office. We were both unhappy. Apparently Van had detected this in my daily demeanor. One day, while sitting at my desk working away, Van approached me and said, "Charlie, since you won't be able to start placing any of the steel for another two weeks or so, why don't you take the next two weeks off and go back to Alabama, and get your family. Don't worry about any loss of any income, your pay will continue on. However, be sure that you save all of your expense slips for the cost of moving your family up here. Keep track of such things as lodging, gas, food and any other expense and drive carefully. I will see to it that you are reimbursed."

I was overjoyed at his instruction. I called Mary Ann immediately. Mary Ann said that she would arrange to have all of our furniture placed in storage; and that she would work through the next day. I told her that I would be leaving Gunnison as soon as I got back to the boarding house to pick up my clothing. The two of us, being young and impetuous never gave a thought to where we would live once we arrived back in Gunnison. I had, however, checked with the school where our boys would be attending. I met with their teachers and was satisfied that the boys would be in good hands at school. Edward would be in the third grade and Arnold would be in the first grade.

We had discussed the possibility of buying a trailer to live in, but we had not really decided on exactly what we would do. I left Gunnison in mid-afternoon headed back to Alabama to get the family. I followed the same procedure as I had when I left Alabama. I didn't make any unnecessary stops, other than for gas and food. In those days I could drive all day and night without stopping for sleep. On the third day of traveling, I arrived at our house in Birmingham. Mary Ann and the boys came running out to the truck to greet me. Mary Ann had everything packed, and was ready for me to start loading things into the truck. The storage people were due out that day to pick up our furniture. They arrived at 10 that morning and began taking the furniture out of the house, loading it onto their moving van. That same evening, November 22, 1962, we began our journey to Colorado.

Mary Ann would drive our car with the kids, and I would drive the truck. Both vehicles were in top condition. The car was our 1958 Oldsmobile. On our way out of Birmingham, we stopped by to see my folks. We gave them the keys to our house, and informed them that we might put the house up for sale, depending on how things went with us. There was lots of hugging and kissing going before we left their house. They sure hated to see us leave.

I was driving in front of Mary Ann and the boys as we headed out of town to our new adventure in the Rocky Mountains of Colorado. We had only been traveling for about three hours when I pulled over at this motel. Mary Ann pulled right in behind me. I was pretty much fatigued by this time, so, I suggested that we eat dinner, stay overnight at this motel, shower, and get a full nights rest before proceeding on with our journey. This was what we did.

The next morning we started out at dawn and had only

been driving for an hour or so when I noticed Mary Ann blinking the headlights of the car, a prearranged signal for me to pull over and stop. Mary Ann said that we should stop at the nearest place for breakfast, because the kids were getting pretty hungry.

We would often pull off on the side of the road to view some of the wonderful scenery. The kids took turns riding with Mary Ann and then with me. On our second day out, we stopped for lunch, and talked about where we might live. Once we arrived in Gunnison. I suggested that we stop in Pueblo, Colorado and buy a trailer. That way we would be sure to have a nice place to live. It was okay with Mary Ann. So, when we arrived in Pueblo, we searched out the places that sold house trailers (today called mobile homes). We came upon a dealership and were, of course, greeted by this smiling salesman. He showed us several of the top-line trailers. We selected a Skyline, which was 12 ft. wide and 60 ft long. The dealer agreed to deliver and set the trailer up for only a $150.00 fee, a very good deal I thought. They had told us that it would take approximately three days for delivery. We spent the night in a motel there in Pueblo.

The next day we stopped by the place where we bought the trailer and saw that they were getting everything ready to make the delivery to Gunnison. The Salesman suggested that I call ahead, using their phone, to reserve a place to park our trailer when it arrived. We were also able to finish with the paper work involving the purchase of the trailer.

My memory served me well, because I remembered a trailer court, about 4 blocks from downtown Gunnison. It was called Larsen Trailer Park. I called information for their number.

The owner answered the call, and said, "Yes, we do have some vacant spaces. How large is your trailer? "

I told him the size and he said, "Great. We have a couple spaces that will handle it." He asked to speak with the salesman to confirm that I had bought a trailer and to ask when it would be delivered. He then quoted me a space rental price of $55 a month. Plus, he said, another $50 a month for the water and electricity hook up. It was a great relief to both Mary Ann and me knowing that we would have a nice place to live in Gunnison. We left Pueblo, and soon arrived in Salida for lunch. We passed near Qukay Peak, elevation - 13,955 ft. To our surprise, the roads were clear as crystal, no ice whatsoever. The road departments were continually placing sand on the highway. However, there was lots of snow in those big snow banks alongside the road. The mountains, of course, were covered with deep snow. The temperature was very low. But our vehicles purred along just fine. I was sure glad that I had put in plenty of antifreeze before leaving Birmingham.

As we traveled through this beautiful countryside, we saw a road sign that said there was a rest stop just twenty miles ahead. When we reached the rest stop, we pulled over to rest and stretch for a while. The boys made a little snowman. Then, they started throwing snowballs at each other. They were having the time of their lives. Mary Ann and I let them play, while we were drinking our coffee. I don't remember what kind of coffee it was, but I do remember it tasting so very, good.

We arrived in Gunnison in the late afternoon. We took a motel room until the new trailer arrived. I placed a call to the dealership in Pueblo, to give them our phone number at this motel. The manager of the dealership told me that the driver had already departed Pueblo with our Trailer, but he would call him on the radio to give him our phone number in Gunnison. Upon arrival, he would call us.

The next day, Mary Ann and I took the boys to school. The Principal escorted us to their classrooms, and introduced Edward and Arnold to their teachers and the other students. Edward and Arnold were so delighted, because all of the kids accepted them with a hearty welcome. We then left the school and ate lunch at my favorite little cafe. George wasn't working there any longer; he had been called in to start work on the dam. Edward and Arnold have many times expressed the feeling that they wished we had never left Gunnison, Colorado. The kids loved it there from that very first day.

After completing our tour of Gunnison, we went back to the motel where we were staying. When we arrived, the clerk at the desk informed us that the driver of our trailer had called. The message was that he would be arriving the next day around 3 p.m. I called Van to inform him that I was back in Gunnison. He said, "Good, take your time in getting set up, call me when you get settled in."

Next we went to the Larson Trailer Park to introduce ourselves to the owner. As I recall, he was a very nice gentleman. He showed us the space that he had reserved for us. He assured us that as soon as the trailer arrived that he would have the electrician come over and hook it up. We signed all the necessary papers that were involved in renting this space and paid our rent money up front.

The next day our trailer didn't arrive at 3 p.m., as promised. The driver called and said that due to the heavy snowfall he had been unable to travel over the pass. He would be forced to wait, until the road department had cleared the roads. However, he did estimate that he would be arriving the next day around just before noon. We stayed at the Motel another night.

The next morning about 9:30 a.m., we received a call from the driver informing us that our trailer had arrived. He had been able to arrive it sooner than he had expected. The owner of the trailer park showed him where to park our trailer. After breakfast, we met the driver at the park. Everything had been set up really well within three hours. That evening, we unloaded our stuff into the trailer and prepared the beds for a good nights sleep in our new home.

The next morning, we woke up in our new home only to discover that there had been a heavy snowfall and it was still in progress. We were rather lucky to have gotten moved in when we did. Our trailer was nice and warm and so were we. We all got dressed and went to have breakfast at our favorite little cafe. In my opinion, they served the best meals in town. In town, the snowplows were going up and down the streets, clearing the snow from the main part of Gunnison. But the snow continued to fall. It was a spectacular sight to see those big snowflakes coming down and so much snow on the ground. The boys couldn't wait to get out in it and make another snowman.

Mary Ann though it would be a good idea to stop at J.C. Penny's and buy some heavy down jackets for herself and the boys. She also bought some heavy winter socks, snow boots, fur lined gloves, and nice warm caps lined with fur, to keep their little heads and ears warm. We also bought two small toboggans, one for each of the boys. After we finished our shopping, we went to one of the hills there in Gunnison, so the boys could try out their new sleds. We all had a ball but, of course, they didn't want to leave.

On the way back to the trailer park, I stopped by the Goodyear store, and bought four new steel-studded tires for my truck, and made arrangements for Mary Ann to stop by the next day to have four new snow tires put on her car. The next morning, Mary Ann took the boys to attend their first day of school and it was time for me to get back on the job. When I arrived at the job site I was informed that a delivery of steel would be arriving in two days. So, I had to get busy calling the Union Hall for a crew of Rodmen.

After completing my daily activities on the job, I departed for home. I found the boys playing outside with the neighborhood kids when I got there. I asked them how their first day at school had been. They both said it had been great.

They continued playing with their little friends with whom they had become acquainted at school. Most of the kids in the park were in the same grades as Edward and Arnold. Inside, Mary Ann was busy putting things away. She had really worked hard and fast that first day putting things in their proper places. She even had the pictures placed on the walls. I could sense that she was tired so, I suggested that we eat out, and she quickly agreed with me. I finished taking my shower and her and the boys were already to go out for dinner. We ate at a different restaurant that evening, and their food was excellent, too. Everyone was very nice. Deep down I could sense that we were going to enjoy living in Gunnison.

The next day I was expecting to greet a crew of Rodmen when I arrived at work. To my surprise, there was a message on my desk for me to call the Ironworkers Business Agent in

Denver. When I got through to him, he said, "Due to the heavy work load in the Denver area, I'm not able to send any people to your job." I gasped, "What am I supposed to do? Where am I going to find the rodmen I need?"

He told me that he had already contacted the Business Agent of the International Rod Carriers Building & Common Laborers Union in Grand Junction, and that they would supply the necessary people that I would need for this project. The only drawback was that I would have to train these people to tie steel. I didn't think I was ready for this kind of experience. I briefed Van on the situation, and he said, "Well, Charlie, we have one thing going for us. They won't be placing any steel for at least another five weeks. You should have enough time to set up school in the steel yard." I placed a call into the Business Agent at Grand Junction, Local Union No. 813, requesting that he send five young, energetic people to the Blue Mesa Dam. He told me that he understood my frustration, and that he would work with me in every way possible.

I spent the rest of the day with our Structural Engineer, (Ron Petty) sitting up false work, which is the temporary structure erected to support work in the process of construction. It consists of shoring or vertical posting form work for beams and slabs, as well as lateral bracing. I would need this in teaching these people how to tie Re-Bar. (Reinforcing Steel)

I left the job site and a frustrating day, headed for home. Driving along on those winding, Colorado roads, I was thinking about what I was to do. I wasn't even sure if I was qualified to teach these people how to place steel. I knew the tying of steel wouldn't be a problem, but the actual placing, and identifying the bar sizes would be a different story. I thought maybe I should call my friend Charlie Green in Birmingham, and get his opinion about what I should do.

Upon my arrival at home, as usual, I was greeted by my loving wife, and my wonderful boys. Mary Ann had dinner all prepared (Steak, Gravy, and Potatoes.) After dinner, Mary Ann could sense the kind of a day that I'd had. She asked me about the problem. I explained to her what had taken place, and that I was thinking about calling Charlie Green to seek his advice. She said, "Oh honey, I didn't want to tell you the bad news about what happened to Charlie Green, during our trip to Gunnison." I said, "What do you mean? What happened to Charlie Green?"

Charlie's hobby was fishing. Come hell or high water, Charlie would go fishing whenever he could. It was his greatest pleasure. Apparently, while I was in Colorado, he had gone fishing, but I guess it was the wrong time of the year to be fishing. Mary Ann explained that Charlie was standing at the stream fishing, when he was approached by a game warden who asked Charlie to stop fishing and leave the area. Charlie displayed a fit of anger and had reached into his back pocket for his wallet to show the game warden that he had a permit to fish in this particular area. Maybe, partly because of the hostile attitude Charlie had displayed, the game warden thought that Charlie was reaching for a gun. In a split second of terrible misjudgment, the warden pulled out his gun and shot Charlie and killed him on the spot. I was dumfounded. This was a terrible shock to me. I could hardly believe it when Mary Ann told me.

Charlie was the kind of person who was always fair and honest with all people. He realized that management was in the drivers' seat when it came to hiring and firing of Ironworkers. I remember him telling some of the Ironworkers he dispatched out to various jobs, that he was in the position of getting them a job, but he wasn't in the position of keeping the job for them. It would be up to the Ironworker to keep his job. Words of truth from an honest man. (Later on, I found out that the game warden had been tried and convicted of manslaughter for the death of Charlie Green. Since it was not premeditated, the warden received a sentence of only six years in prison.)

The next day at work, the five men that I had requested from the Union Hall greeted me. They seemed to be okay guys. They were very pleasant, and seemed to be willing to learn the steel business. One of the guys told me that he had worked a little bit placing Re-Bar, but not very much. They didn't have any of the right tools for the job, but we had anticipated this. The day before, Ron Petty had placed a call to their main office in Dallas, Texas, requesting an immediate shipment of the required tools. That evening, the tools arrived by Federal Express.

I took the crew over to the steelyard, where we had everything ready for them to start learning how to tie steel. After showing them how to install the tie wire in the Ideal Reels, I started them off with the most common and most often used tie of them all, which is known as the snap tie. I had them practice tying the snap tie for the rest of the day. At the end of the shift, I checked back in with the guys to see how they were doing. To my surprise, they had done real well. They complained about blisters on their hands, but their attitude was that they weren't about to give up. I was pleased.

The next day a truckload of re-bar arrived. Before the truck could be unloaded, I had to have a bulldozer come in with a blade and clear the snow away from where we were going to stack the re-bar. The weather was getting worse and there had been a heavy snowfall the night before. The temperature on this day was 15 degrees below zero. That's cold. However, the wind wasn't blowing, which made it at least tolerable. We had cribbing at hand four feet high onto which we could lay the re-bar. We couldn't lay it on the ground, because the snow would cover it up, and it would be hard to identify. By evening the crew had gotten it all stacked and organized.

I was pleased with this crew of men. They were conscientious, willing to work and learn. I got to know them very well, and understand their needs. They were all married with kids, and each one of them had a strong desire to make something of themselves. There wasn't a smart-mouth in the bunch. They were not like some ironworkers that I know today. Over the next few weeks, these men showed great progress. They had mastered the art of tying re-bar. They had learned how to identify the bar sizes quite well, too.

I began to spend more time in the Engineering Department. Ron was teaching me how to detail re-bars. We were also making templates for the bar supports that were to be used in the diversion tunnels. Things were beginning to click in my mind, to come together. Here I was a Superintendent, but without a foreman anywhere. I would have to be the one directly in charge of placing the Re-Bar. I soon realized what lay ahead of me. And believe me, I wasn't too happy. I could see the writing on the wall.

The day finally arrived for us to start placing the re-bar in the tunnels, and as it turned out, we had to call in about ten more men to get the work done. The five men I had trained were a great asset to me. Without them, I would never have made it. The first week, we worked only 40 hours per week, and the second week, we worked only 40 hours per week. From there on out, it hit the fan. I was working anywhere from 60 to 80 hours per week. I pleaded with the Union to try and find me a foreman. But no luck. There were times when as soon as I got home, I was called to come back to the job site, for some stupid correction the Bureau of Reclamation wanted taken care of before the next pour. The other aggravating thing was that the workers were making more money than I was. They were being paid for all overtime at time and a half, and here I was on a straight salary of only $195.00 per week. This I hadn't anticipated.

This torture continued on for the next several months. I become pretty exhausted, and submitted my resignation to the company. They asked that I withdraw my resignation, and they convinced me to stay on to complete the job. After that, my hours were reduced back to a normal 40 hours per week. However, this taught me a great lesson. I would never accept a job with a salary and would always work by the hour, and demand to be paid for all overtime.

During our stay in Gunnison, Mary Ann and I were invited out on many occasions to parties, dances, and other social events. Luckily a friend of ours had a teenage daughter, who enjoyed baby-sitting. We always called on her when we went out for an evening. She was a terrific babysitter and the boys loved her. We trusted her judgment and kindness. Mary Ann had taken a job at the local bank in Gunnison as a secretary, so, before long, we became acquainted with a lot of people in Gunnison and needed babysitting more often.

As the Dam project in Gunnison was winding down, Joe Wheeler, who was our project manager, had accepted a job with the Bethel Corporation of California to serve as project manager on another dam project in Eugene, Oregon. Since my portion of the work was nearing completion, I placed a call to Joe, inquiring about the possibility of my working on this project with him. He told me to come on out and get signed up. So when I finished with the loose ends on the Blue Mesa Dam project, I would set out for California.

Chapter 8

CALIFORNIA

Mary Ann and I decided that she and the boys would remain in Gunnison until the school year was over. We parted reluctantly. I drove our car to California and left Mary Ann with the truck. On my way to Stanton, California, where the main office was located, I had to go through San Jose, California. This gave me the opportunity to visit with Mary Ann's sister Bernice and her family. Bernice's husband's name was Ed Samson, and their son's name was Bobby. Bobby was six months older than our Arnold was.

I remember the drive from Gunnison to San Jose as being very beautiful. The mountains were filled with beautiful golden grasses. It was breathtaking. Ed mentioned that San Jose Steel Co. had advertised for a person of my experience, so, I called them and set up an interview. The interview was successful. I was hired. I called my friend Joe, in Stanton, informing him of my decision to take the job in San Jose. He wished me luck and told me, that if I ever needed a job, just to give him a call. I called Mary Ann to tell her that we were moving to San Jose and she was pleased.

The very next day after my interview with San Jose Steel, I started to work on a telephone building right in downtown San Jose. The first couple of weeks I stayed with Bernice and Ed. But after two weeks with relatives, I found out that it was neither healthy nor wise. So, I rented an apartment at the San Jose City College dormitory for only $1.00 per day. "What a deal."

Mary Ann and I talked to each other every night. I really missed her and the boys. During the weekends I visited the surrounding areas of California. I was really impressed, because it is such a beautiful State, and warm! When it came time for Mary Ann and the boys to come out to California, I made arrangements with San Jose Steel to take time off to drive back to Colorado to get my family.

Mary Ann had found a buyer for our trailer. She loaded everything into the truck and away she went. We met up approximately 150 miles west of Gunnison. We swapped vehicles. Mary Ann drove the car and I drove the truck. I told her that we would have to stop at the next big town, so that we could buy new tires for the vehicles. They were wearing bald.

When we arrived in San Jose, we went directly to the furnished apartment that I had rented directly across the street from Bernice and Ed's apartment. Mary Ann's Brother, Bill and his family from Seattle were visiting with Bernice. Arnold assisted me unloading our stuff. We unloaded everything into the apartment and all went out with Bernice, Bill, and family to eat dinner. Then we went directly back to our apartment and went to bed. We were really exhausted from the trip. The next morning, I went back to work, and Mary Ann arranged the apartment very nicely. The boys were getting acquainted with the neighborhood kids and playing with their cousin, Bobby.

We lived in that apartment for only one month before one became vacant in the same complex where Ed and Bernice lived. It was a nice two-bedroom unit with a view. There was also a swimming pool in the complex. Ed and Bernice were the managers of this apartment building. The boys really enjoyed the swimming pool, and so did we. The boys had already enrolled in school, but they didn't seem to like the school in San Jose as well as they had liked the one in Gunnison. The majority of the kids were Hispanic, and primarily hung out with their own kind. They weren't friendly by any means towards newcomers, especially, white kids. However, Edward and Arnold were very determined little boys. They developed friendships with lots of the white kids and Hispanic kids.

I worked in the field with San Jose Steel for approximately 6 months when they were awarded the job of placing the re-bar on the Yuba Bear Project Dam, in Grass Valley, California. Grass Valley is approximately 25 miles northeast of Sacramento. Its elevation is 8,749 ft. and it can get quite cold. I thought Colorado was cold, but it was nothing compared to this place. I thought California was going to be warm.

Ben Painter, who was the Chief Estimator for San Jose Steel, offered me the job of detailing this project. One of the conditions would be that I would have to live in Grass Valley during the week. It was a 40-hour per week job. The detailer that was on the job had submitted his resignation, so they needed some one to take his place. My responsibilities were to coordinate the sequence of deliveries and to transpose the concept of the master plans on to Bethlehem Steel's detail sheets. Bethlehem Steel was the vendor fabricating and supplying the re-bar for the project.

Mary Ann encouraged me to take the job, knowing it would further my education and experience. I accepted the offer, and departed for Grass Valley. The incumbent detailer, Joe Frost, greeted me. He took me around the project site, so that I would become acquainted with the area. Paul Hardman was the General Contractor. I was introduced to all of his staff. It was similar to the project in Colorado; only this project was much larger.

Paul Hardman was in dire need of a Carpenter Foreman, so I placed a call to my old buddy, Bob Allen, in Colorado to see if he would be interested in the job. He said that he was, so I gave him the name and phone number of the person to talk to. One week later, Bob showed up on the job site. He had accepted their offer and he started to work immediately. I felt good that I was able to repay him for my job in Colorado.

I had rented a two-bedroom apartment in Grass Valley, so, Bob asked if he could share it with me. We split the cost, of course. Bob's family had moved to Mary Annville, California and he went home on the weekends to be with them. I would also go home on most of the weekends to be with my family.

There were times when Mary Ann and the boys would drive up to Grass Valley to spend the weekend with me.

After about six months, I became dissatisfied with this job. I couldn't stand being cooped up all day in that tiny job trailer. There was no one to talk with and I spent most of my time drafting, or talking on the telephone. Every once in a while one of Hardman's Engineers would stop by, but only to put a question regarding the job. I also missed the daily life with my family. A few hours on the weekend was too short a time to be with them and then go back to the empty apartment in Grass Valley.

I called Ben Painter to inform him of my disenchantment. I told him that I wanted to come back to San Jose to work in the field. He agreed, but he told me that I would probably have to wait about two weeks before he could find someone to replace me. I was going to be able wait two weeks.

To my delight, my replacement arrived on the job the next week. His name was Carl Bellingham. He was a much older person than I was, and he really knew his stuff. I finished out the week with him, and I headed back to San Jose. On Sunday evening, I received a call from our Field Superintendent, Joe Frista. He welcomed me back, and gave me directions to the job that I was to report to the next day. I was so glad to be back with my family.

We decided to move from the Fairlane Apartments. We rented a nice three-bedroom house on McKee Road, which was just down the street from the apartments. Edward, Arnold, and Bobby were still able to see each other and play with one another everyday after school. One day, Mary Ann and the boys had gone shopping in downtown San Jose. They came to a pet store. In the front window was this little white snowball puppy, barking away and waging his tail. Mary Ann and the boys fell in love with that puppy at first sight. She bought the puppy, for the boys, of course. The puppy was a male Laso Apso. We named him Nikie. Nikie lived with us for the next 18 years as a part of our family.

After a short while I became even more dissatisfied,

working for San Jose Steel then I had been in Grass Valley, so, I quit and went to work for Bethlehem Steel in South San Francisco. I was employed in the engineering department as a steel detailer. During my stay with Bethlehem Steel, I became much more educated in the steel business. Arnold Peppin was my supervisor, and his assistant was Robert Dugan. I really enjoyed working with them. They were a great team. I have always regretted having to leave them, but the pay wasn't that good. There was another factor, too. Mary Ann had become pregnant, so, I had to look for work that paid more money.

While I was working at Bethlehem Steel, I became well acquainted with most of the Steel Placers in the area. I put the word out that I was seeking work in the field as a foreman. I received several offers, but I chose Murphy Steel over them all, because Murphy's offer was the best. Their offer consisted of a guarantee of 40 hours per week, rain or shine. Anything over 40 hours, I would be paid double time. I also was issued the use of a new company truck, and a company credit card for all gas and related expenses. Also Murphy Steel was the largest placer of Bethlehem Steel's Re-Bar.

Vern Valadka, was the General Field Superintendent for Murphy Steel. He was in his late 60's. Whenever there was a problem with the detailing of some of his jobs, he would always come through Bethlehem Steel's detailing department to inquire about the cause of the problem. This was how I became acquainted with him. Arnold Peppin made me feel real good one day when he told me that Vern was always happy when he knew that I would be the one detailing his jobs. Mainly, he said, because I made fewer mistakes.

My first job for Murphy was a pier job in San Francisco. The pier was huge, over a mile long. Manson General, from Seattle was the General Contractor. Walter F. Peterson was the project manager for Manson. On this first job I had the blueprints completely memorized, because I had been the one who detailed it, while working at Bethlehem. This gave me more time to spend supervising the crew.

Murphy's bid for placing this job was $32.00 per ton.

Vern told me that he knew it would be a difficult job for me to bring in under $32.00 a ton. He also told me that he didn't have another foreman who would be able to place it at that price. As we chatted, he told me that he anticipated the cost would run around $46.00 per ton. He let me know that he and the owner of Murphy Steel were really dissatisfied with the estimator who had estimated this job, but that it was to late for them to back out of the bid.

I knew from experience that the first job you do for a company usually is the one that sets your reputation. Even so, I put my reputation on the line by quoting a $16.00 per ton placing price on the job to Vern. He said, "Now, Chuck, let's be realistic. I have been in this business for 50 years and I have never seen anyone who could place Re-Bar that cheap."

I said, "Vern, if you'll let me choose my own crew, and provide me with the equipment I need, I can assure you that I will place this job for $16.00 a ton or less. If I don't succeed, I'll forfeit a full weeks pay, and seek work elsewhere." I put out my hand, and asked, "Do we have a deal?" Vern took my hand, shook it and said, "Deal!"

Vern had detected from the sound of my voice, and the look in my eye, that I was very serious in my commitment. He was very curious and asked, " Chuck, I know that you're a smart man, so, please clue me in as to just how the hell you propose to do this unheard of thing." I told Vern that I had given the problem a great deal of thought and I wasn't just popping off. I reminded him that I knew the Shop Foreman at Bethlehem Steel fairly well and he had agreed to ship and deliver the steel, as we needed it. That way, the steel could be taken directly off the truck and placed adjacent to where it was to be placed. This would completely eliminate the need to handle it twice or store it. Then I told him about the spray paint I planned to use that would replace the Knell (a crayon type of marker) that was normally used. This would be another time saving element. I had also arranged for the use of a crane from Manson, so the steel could be lifted off the truck and not just dropped on the ground. Vern was impressed with my plan and wished me good luck.

I started placing phone calls to various Rod busters that I had known in the San Jose area. The first man I hired was a fellow by the name of Elwood Moore. El would serve as my Lieutenant throughout this entire job. In other words, he would be my right-hand man for the entire job. One of the other people I hired was a Hawaiian, whom I had worked with before in San Jose. Even though his first name was David, he preferred being called "Pineapple." Finally I had the crew of men assembled that I knew would support me in making my commitment come true.

Mary Ann was, in the meantime, getting bigger and bigger, so, we decided to move from the house on McKee road. Mary Ann had been house hunting, since we would need more room when the baby arrived. She found a nice house to rent at 14810 McVay Blvd. in San Jose. This was a roomy home, located in a very nice neighborhood on a quaint hillside. All of the neighbors greeted us warmly. When we'd lived there for a month or so, I was invited to join the neighborhoods poker club. Once a month, we would meet at one another's house and play poker. We really had lots of fun. (I had learned my lesson earlier. Poker was for fun, not money.)

Things were working out swell for us again. I had a great job, a wonderful, supporting wife, two bright, healthy young boys and a new baby on the way. I had the world by the tail. After the first month on my new job, Vern asked that I submit a tonnage report indicating how many tons we had placed during the previous month. They would then invoice accordingly. I knew that we were doing real well, and I couldn't wait to submit my first report.

On one warm day, Vern and the owner, Rich Murphy came driving up to the job site. They both got out of the car and approached me. Vern introduced Rich to me, and Rich said, "Chuck, I am very pleased to meet you. I couldn't believe the tonnage report that you submitted for last months billing, are you sure you didn't make a mistake?"

I said, "Yes." I then opened my brief case to show him the weight slips from Bethlehem.

He was truly amazed, and said, "You know when Vern had told me of your quote, I said to him, well Vern; it looks like you have a very unrealistic person working for you. I thought you were nuts. But from the looks of the job, it looks as if you were right. Do you realize what your cost was for this past month?

I told him I had a rough idea.

He said, "Right to the penny, it was $14.89 per ton. Chuck, this is great, keep up the good work. I really appreciate your being aboard."

The Company's policy was to mail all employees' paychecks to their homes, rather than deliver them to the job sites. The paychecks were always delivered and received on Friday of each week. In my next paycheck, after having met Rich Murphy, there was a substantial raise. I got a 15% increase in my wages. They really treated me well. It was their way of sharing the profit of my labor.

My costs remained consistent throughout the entire job. I was really on a roll in the eyes of my employer. I could do nothing wrong, which did cause some resentment among some of the other foremen. Here I was, a new kid on the block, and had been given a new company truck and a company credit card, among other benefits, as well as a nice raise in pay for my efforts. I wasn't too concerned with the jealousy of others. I wasn't about to let anything stand in my way of achieving my ultimate goal in life, to be a top field superintendent or, possibly, to start my own company.

I had worked hard, and had done my homework. On several occasions, Rich Murphy would stop by the job and invite me to have lunch with him. We discussed the jobs that were coming up, and he picked my brain. One day he said, "Vern is getting on in years and will be retiring with in a year or so. Chuck, if you continue with your outstanding attitude, while making the company money, his job will be yours."

Vern recognized my ability to comprehend and decipher architectural drawings. He usually stopped by and asked for my help when he had a question regarding some details on the drawings. He said many times, "Chuck, you really know how to work with me, and I really do appreciate it. All of the guys in my crew were working well, too. So, I suggested to Vern that they be paid above Union Scale, and he agreed. I thought, what is a leader without the men under him? These men were punctual, loyal, and performed up to and beyond my expectations each and every day.

The time for Mary Ann to deliver the new baby was getting nearer and nearer. We didn't know whether our baby would be a boy or girl. I was hoping for a girl, and if it were, then we would call it quits, and have no more kids. Three would be enough. After all, Mary Ann and I were young enough to grow up with them. Before Mary Ann became pregnant, she was always busy, taking the boys back and forth to play little league baseball, and attending their school and church activities during the day. She was always ready to support the boys in whatever they chose to do. Even during the full term of her pregnancy, she was a real trooper, always there for them and me. I never heard her complain about the messes that the boys and I created in the house, such as, leaving our underwear, socks, and clothes lying scattered willy-nilly around the house. She would always pick up after us. She would also rise before us in the mornings to have my lunch and breakfast prepared for my day's work.

Chapter 9

CHRISTINA

In the early morning of August 3, 1965, Mary Ann's water broke. So I immediately called my office to inform them that I wouldn't be into work on this day. The boys were left to care for themselves; they were old enough, and big enough, to do so. I placed a call to Mary Ann' sister, Bernice, to inform her that Mary Ann's time was at hand. We arrived at the San Jose Hospital and Mary Ann was placed on a gurney and rolled into the delivery room.

Dr. Wade was Mary Ann's Physician; the head Nurse in Delivery placed a call to him to inform him that Mary Ann would probably be ready to deliver in mid-afternoon. The Nurse had said to me, "The doctor's instructions are to prep Mary Ann for a Transsacral (Caudal) Block." I wanted to be present during the delivery, but Mary Ann and all concern objected. I never could understand why fathers were not allowed in delivery to witness the birth of their own child.

"A Transsacral (Caudal) Block produces anesthesia of the perineum and, occasionally, the lower abdomen. An addition to obstetric anesthesia has been an adaptation of the caudal block. This is analogous to the change from a single-injection spinal to a serial spinal. A malleable needle or a nylon uterine catheter is inserted into the caudal canal. This is allowed to remain in place and is attached by a tube to a reservoir of anesthetic solution. When the woman in labor complains of pain, an injection is made, and subsequent injections are given as indicated." (Qtd.

in 2nd Edition, Medical Surgical Nursing, Brunner, Emerson, Ferguson, Suddarth on page 122.)

On this beautiful, glorious, day, August 3, 1965 at 5: 03 pm, I was presented with a most precious gift. Mary Ann had given birth to our baby girl. I was in the waiting room trying to be nonchalant, prepared to accept whatever the child might be, boy or girl. I prayed that Mary Ann and our baby would be in good health; and Lord, if it be thy will, let it be a little girl. When the nurse came through the waiting room with our newly born baby, she informed me that it was a baby girl. I thanked God for his blessing.

I asked the nurse how Mary Ann was doing. She said, "She is doing well, however, it was a hard delivery for her." I wondered for a few moments at this little girl before me, but then hurried into the delivery room to be with Mary Ann. She was still groggy from the anesthesia. The nurse told us that she would be groggy for some time. I knelt down and kissed her, and whispered into her ear that I loved her, and that our baby was a little girl.. I told her that I would be leaving the hospital to go home to inform the boys about their baby sister but would return right away.

When I arrived at the house, the boys weren't there, so, I called Bernice to see if they were at her place and she said that they were. They had ridden their bikes to her place, and were having dinner with Bobby. I informed her of the birth of our baby girl, and she shouted over the phone, "Thank God, it's about time!" I could hear her telling the boys about the birth of their baby sister. I told Bernice that after I had finished taking a shower, I would be down to see them.

When I arrived at Bernice's, the boys began asking how Mom was doing, and when would she be coming home. I said, in a few days. I explained to Bernice about the Caudal Block. While I was at Bernice's, I used her phone to call Helen and Margaret in Seattle. They were happy for us. Leona said that she had never known me to be so excited before. Then, I called my parents to inform them of the birth. Bernice invited the boys to spend the night with Bobby.

I went back to the hospital to join Mary Ann, and our baby daughter. When I arrived, Mary Ann had already been taken to her room. When I entered the room, the baby was cuddled in its mommy arms. I kissed them both, and asked Mary Ann how she was feeling?

"It was tough, but worth every ounce of the pain." She said.

I stayed with them until they slumbered off into dreamland. I kissed them both goodnight, and told Mary Ann that I would return the next day. When I left the hospital, I was on cloud nine. We had been blessed with a healthy baby girl and I thanked God all the way home.

From all of the excitement, I wasn't able to sleep, so I put on a pot of coffee, and sat down to watch TV. I kept dozing off while sitting in my leather recliner. In that twilight zone between wake and sleep, it seemed I kept hearing a voice intoning, "Be prepared, the worst is yet to come." This occurred several times during the early morning hours. I suddenly came awake about 4:30 a.m. I jumped out of my chair, and remember saying to myself, Oh! My God, I am late for work. My mind was totally blank. At this time I didn't even remember that Mary Ann had given birth to our baby girl.

I remember putting my work clothes and boots on and running out to my truck. I left in a panic. I stopped, and bought a doughnut, and a cup of coffee, and away I went. I was about to drive onto the Bay Shore freeway, when all of a sudden a small bright orange ball of light appeared on the hood of my truck. It wasn't until then that I realized I should be going to the hospital to see Mary Ann and our baby. I began to break out in a cold sweat. I immediately turned into another direction, and headed toward the hospital.

It was only 5:15 am when I arrived at the hospital. I remember saying to myself, this is too early to wake up Mary Ann, so I turned around and went back home. I felt like an idiot. I called Vern to inform him of our blessing, and asked him, if it would be okay for me to take the rest of the week off, and, of course, he said that it would be okay.

I took a cold shower, trying to regain my senses. I didn't understand what my lapse of awareness meant or what that ominous voice signified. I felt just as I had in combat, helping to pick up the blown out guts of my dead comrades while I had placed their organs back onto their bodies, so that all of their remains would remain intact. It was a very strange feeling that came over me. I was disoriented.

After I had gotten dressed, I went to pick up Edward and Arnold, so I could take them with me to see their mommy and baby sister. When we arrived at the hospital, Mary Ann and baby sister were doing fine. The boys were smiling, and they hugged and kissed mommy and baby sister. Bernice asked me to tell Mary Ann that she would be in to see her later on in the day. Mary Ann was a little bit upset with me, because of the way that I was dressed. I was only wearing a white tee shirt, and a pair of pants. Of course, I didn't see anything wrong with the way that I was dressed. I was proud of my well-developed physique. But I did understand, I should have at least put a nice sport shirt on, and I don't know why I didn't before leaving the house. I still felt strange.

Since I had the most say-sos, in naming the boys, I left the naming of our baby girl entirely up to Mary Ann. She had chosen the name, "Christina Margaret Herring." And so on that date, which was August 4, 1965, that name was entered onto her Birth Certificate. Mary Ann and I both were 33 years of age when our daughter was born.

That evening, Bernice, Ed, and Bobby came to visit with Mary Ann, and to welcome Chris into the family. Bernice really became attached to Christina. They brought Mary Ann a big bouquet of Roses, which brightened up her day.

After three days in the hospital, Mary Ann and Chris were released to go home. In the mid-afternoon, I picked them up, and took them home. Before we could even get out of the car, most of the neighbors came over to welcome Mary Ann, and to extend their congratulations on the birth of Chris. They had already given Mary Ann a baby shower, but they presented her with more gifts. This was really a great neighborhood.

Sometime over the next few days, Mary Ann came down with what is known as Bell's palsy. Bell's Palsy is a peripheral facial weakness attended by aching pain near the angle of the jaw or behind the ear. In her case, it was the 7th nerve involvement on the left side of her face. She was totally paralyzed on the left side of her face for approximately three months. She could only talk from the right side of her mouth. I felt the agony she was going through. In those days, the doctors weren't sure how to treat, or even know what caused the paralysis.

I knew there were times when she would be all alone, weeping and feeling the burden that had been placed upon her. Could this have been the fulfillment of the premonition spoken to me, "the worst is yet to come?" I continued working every day, but I decided that I would fix my own lunches, instead of Mary Ann having to get out of bed so early. From that day forward, I started waiting on myself, rather than having Mary Ann do for me. She had enough on her plate with Chris and the Bell's palsy as it was. But even with her ailment, she never showed any signs of distress. She always saw to it that the boys got off to school, fit as a fiddle.

The Bell's palsy disappeared after a few months, and our lives were beginning to get back to normal. We traded our 1958 Oldsmobile in for a new 1965 Plymouth Fury Station Wagon. It was the consensus of our family that we become involved in camping out at some of the beautiful campgrounds in California. We bought tents and all the necessary gear and tackle that we would need to camp out.

Our first trip in our new station wagon was to Seattle, to visit all of our relatives there. Chris would get a little carsick at times, so we would always pull over and rest for a while, until she began to feel better. We had taken a plane trip back to Birmingham to visit with my family. Flying didn't seem to brother her as much as riding in a car did.

When Chris was about three months old, Mary Ann detected a clicking noise on the right side of her hip when she would crawl around. So, she took her to see Dr. Wade, who had delivered her, and right away he x-rayed her little hip. The x-rays showed signs of her hip being dislocated to a certain extent. So, she was given a brace to wear between her legs, in hopes that it would correct the situation. Time and time again, Mary Ann would take her back to see this group of doctors. And time and time again, they would continue to x-ray her from all different angles.

Finally, as she grew older, she didn't have to use the brace any longer, and she began to walk very well. She was growing into a beautiful little girl, but then I might be prejudice. We all loved her with all of our hearts. She was a little on the spoiled side, but I didn't care. She could have anything she wanted. Christina and her mommy were very close. She really loved her brothers. She always called Edward, (Eddy) and Arnold, (Arnie). She used to say that Arnold was too argumentative, and that he wouldn't let her have her way, but Edward would. Her Aunt Bernice would also give her anything she wanted. She really enjoyed going to Bernice's house where she would pull everything out of the drawers, especially her jewelry.

When Chris was a two year old, my folks drove out from Alabama to visit with us, but they couldn't find our address, so they called from a gas station. We drove over to where they were and guided them back to our house. During the short drive, Chris became real pale, and complained of feeling dizzy. But after we got back home and out of the car, she began to feel better. We thought she might be coming down with a cold, like the other kids in the neighborhood.

My folks stayed with us for a week before going back to Alabama. Chris really enjoyed their visit. When it was time for them to leave, Chris wished them a happy and safe trip back to Alabama. She told them to come back anytime. For a two-year old, she was great with words. She was a very bright child.

Chris was a very happy child. She had become acquainted with some of the neighborhood kids her own age and they used to come over and play with her. She always referred to them as being her little friends. On her birthdays, Mary Ann and Bernice would have a birthday party for her at our house. All of her little friends would come over and bring gifts. She was always so excited about receiving and opening gifts. Ed, Bernice, and Bobby would always come over every Friday night, and bring doughnuts. We would have a ball. Sometimes they would bring a large Pizza. Chris would always look out of the window, expecting their visit.

My second job with Murphy was the San Mateo Hayward Bridge, in Hayward, California. This was a very good job for me. I had it well organized. I had the same crew that I had always had. We really made money for Murphy. Things were going well for us at home, too. We had done some camping. The boys were doing very well in school. Edward had become a real good baseball player. Arnold was a real scholar. Edward was a sophomore in High School at James Lick High in San Jose, and baseball was the highlight of his life. He attended Santa Clara College to learn more about the game of baseball. He was a first baseman. I started back to school, attending San Jose City College at nights, and working during the day. I visualized a bright further for my family. I even had visions of Edward becoming a major league baseball player. I taught him throughout his little league years how to bat and throw like Roger Maris with the Yankees. He would throw right handed, and bat left handed, even though he was right handed. And first base was his position.

Mary Ann and I were saving money to buy a house in San Jose. We figured on making San Jose our home forever. Though it was hidden deep, I'd never totally blocked out of my mind, that strange phenomenon that I had experienced when Chris was born. "Be prepared, the worst is yet to come." I had assumed the ailment in Christina's hip, and Mary Ann's Bell's Palsy was what the voice meant. Little did I know at the time what it really meant.

Chapter 10

When I awoke on this beautiful day, the sunrise was slowly creeping over the mountaintop of Alum Rock. People were rising and turning their lights on. Each glitter in the brown darkness announced life awakening to this day. I was in such a blithe mood. I thought about calling in, and requesting the day off, so that I could spend it with my family. But I didn't.

I was driving to work, from San Jose to Oakland, when a strange abstruse feeling began to insert itself into my day. A noise started clanging from underneath the hood of my truck. I remember thinking, oh, my God, what's wrong now? I pulled over to the side of the freeway, and got out, and raised the hood of the truck. The engine was purring away, the sound had disappeared. All of a sudden that unfocused dark feeling flared beneath my skin. A sepulchral bell seemed to be tolling, "You have been blessed and spared, but God has a need for Christina, she will die of Leukemia." I became very nauseated, and felt like throwing up. I couldn't believe what I was hearing. I got back into the truck and drove into work in a daze. The feeling of dread simmered behind the business of my job. I began to wonder if I was a little mentally bent. I have never spoken of this occurrence to anyone so they wouldn't always be looking at me sideways, until now.

Mary Ann was taking Chris to the doctors, day in and day out. They kept X-raying her little body. She had become anemic. Dr. Wade had referred Chris and all her lab tests to Stanford Hospital. That evening I was shopping for groceries at Rosenberg Super Market, which wasn't too far from our house, and only two blocks from Bernice's apartment, when suddenly Ed, Bernice's husband, came into the store, and said that Mary Ann had called him, and she wanted him to find me and tell me to come home at once. As I paid for the groceries, I asked Ed what she had wanted; he said that she didn't say, but for me to hurry home.

I rushed into the house, leaving the groceries in the truck. Mary Ann informed me that she had received a call from Stanford, requesting we bring Christina in at once. We immediately left for Stanford, which was about a 35-minute drive from San Jose. It was in Palo Alto, California. We checked in and they started performing more tests on Chris. A doctor took us aside and asked Mary Ann and me to step into this little room so we could discuss Christina's situation.

He told us that the results from Christina's entire battery of tests were positive, and that she had Leukemia. The top of my head began to throb; I started crying and couldn't stop for sometime. Mary Ann tried to comfort me, but I was out of control. I immediately went into the room where Chris was, and grabbed her up, holding her in my arms.

Our cheeks were touching; tears were running down my face. Chris said to me, "What's wrong Daddy? Why are you crying?" I couldn't even answer her. I held on to her for dear life.

Eventually, I managed to lay her down and leave the room. I had to tell everyone about her having Leukemia. As I was walking down the hall, that voice inside my head whispered to me, "This is what was meant."

I called Bernice, my parents and everyone in Seattle. They all wept with me. A part of me died on this day. As a matter of fact, I think a part of all of us died on this day. It was the beginning of the end. They wanted to keep Chris overnight. Mary Ann said that she would stay with her while I drove home to inform the boys.

This was a very difficult task for me. I had Edward and Arnold sit down on the couch. I informed them that their baby sister was dying. It was a shock to them. It took some time for this tragedy to sink in. We sat huddled together, stunned, and held each other. They could not even form the questions they wanted to ask. Besides, I had no answers, just questions of my own. The next morning, the boys and I went to the hospital.

As we were walking down the hallway to her room, Chris came running out, in a very cheerful mood, and said, "Hi Eddie and Arnie." Edward said back to her, "Hi little sis, how are you doing?" Arnold hugged and kissed her. She was so glad to see her brothers.

The doctors prescribed some kind of medication for Chris. I don't know what it was, but I had the prescription filled before we left the hospital that evening. We all tried to carry on as usual at home. Chris wasn't aware of the trauma that she was to undergo, nor of what we had been informed. She continued playing with her toys, and hiding from Arnold. She and Arnold would always play hide-and-go-seek with one another.

From this point, our lives wouldn't be the same. We had to make lots of adjustments. We avoided anyone coming around Chris with a cold, for fear her condition might worsen. We all tried to carry on with life as before, yet knew that her condition would probably regress; we would have to live out the inevitable crises that lay ahead. The boys still had to continue on with school, and I had to continue working. Mary Ann had the worst job of all, and I must say that she was the strength of our family throughout this terrible ordeal. She had to be with Chris every day of what life remained for her. Day in and day out she had the responsibility of taking Chris back and forth to Stanford for treatments, struggling to maintain her composure around Chris.

Arnold would continue arguing with Chris, and Edward would continue upholding Chris in whatever she wanted. It was so much fun listening to Arnold and Chris argue. Arnold would always give into her, even though he knew that she was in the wrong. Bernice, Ed, and Bobby continued on coming over to our house ever Friday evening. They always brought some doughnuts and a little surprise for Chris. She always looked forward to seeing them drive up in the driveway. She'd run and say to mommy, "Bees is here, Bees is here."

Helen, (Mary Ann's Mom) came to visit now more than ever. She was always a great comfort and help to Mary Ann. I will never forget her generosity, and her kind heart. Chris really loved her Grandma. Helen, as I have described earlier, was such a great conversationalist, she could debate any subject, and yet, she never got upset if I disagreed with her. She would always say, "Well, you have your opinion, and I have mine; and there is nothing you or anyone else can say that would make me change my mind." Actually, this wasn't quite true as she was more interested in the truth than winning. I don't know what we would have done without her support and love.

Every evening when I would return home from work, Chris would be waiting and watching as I pulled into the driveway. She would be looking out the window. I would always get out of the truck and walk onto the front porch, and ring the doorbell.

She would always yell out, "Nobody's home."

I would say, "Well, okay, I will have to leave and find some other little girl to give this candy to."

She would then open the door, and say, "Ha, Ha, I fooled you, didn't I."

I would pick her up, we would kiss and hug and she would begin searching into my pockets to see what her Daddy had brought her. This was a daily ritual with us.

I was beginning to feel the somatic mutations as well as in my soul, mind, and spirit. I wasn't able to understand what was causing me to feel angry all of the time. I was so protective of Chris. I would even take my anger out on Mary Ann and the boys, and my co-workers. I seem to be losing my powers of concentration, and the ability to coordinate. I was mad at the world, at the universe. All day at work, I would be thinking of my baby; I couldn't wait to get home and spend time with her. I would never see her take ballet, play the piano, go off to school, go to a prom…O God, so much loss! I needed my time with her.

Building the Rapid Transit in Oakland was in progress. Vern had put me in charge of overseeing this job. I had hired my brother, and two of my brothers-in-law to work on this project with me. At this time, I was a very irritable person. One day, I witnessed the three of them standing around; so, I fired the three of them. And believe me, my actions didn't go over too well with the rest of the family. I was right, but I was wrong. I was torn.

Mary Ann would constantly drive to Stanford for Christina's treatments. I was never able to understand her perseverance, her endurance and steadying composure. Mary Ann was and is a person of strong character. She is a person of great understanding and sensitivity. She has a mind like a bear trap. Nothing escapes her. I have always referred to her as my walking encyclopedia. Whenever I am too lazy to look up the meaning of a word (which is often), I always ask her. I always believed that Mary Ann was a spin off of her mother. Mary Ann seemed to have inherited all the best characteristics and made them her own.

However, no two individuals behave exactly alike, and no two persons, sick or well, ever duplicate each other. This is eminently reasonable if we but recall the profound possibilities for variations and differences in the organic endowment and the past experience of people. No situation is exactly the same for any two people, since the interaction between environment and organism is most significant, and no two people bring the same selective perception to any given situation. In all this infinite variety it becomes apparent that interpretation of behavior is no easy matter. We cannot easily judge the meaning of an experience for another, since we always see it in terms of our own experience. Recognition of this fact is the first step in learning to evaluate behavior intelligently. (End of sermonette.)

There were repeated times when I would arrive home from work, and Mary Ann would inform me of the results that she had learned during their visit to Stanford. One time Chris went into remission for about 30 days. And during her remission she would seem as normal as any other healthy child without Leukemia. We would rejoice with Bernice, Ed, and Bobby. We would take Chris shopping, and the law was that she could buy anything she desired. We loved those days of happiness, and tried to avoid the inevitable that was deep within.

I was beginning to become more and more hostile with life and the people surrounding me. I was subconsciously, putting the blame for Chris's illness on God. It seemed to be a punishment that was greater than I could bear. I knew that the Paraclete had never touched me, nor did I accept his spirit as comforter. However, I knew that my soul had reached into a state of nihilism, and was seeking the cessation of desires, craving or passion. I didn't know which way to turn. I did know that I would have given my life to spare Chris's life.

About this time I vividly recalled a striking image of a little girl that was about the same age as Chris during my stay in Korea. I was sitting in the back of an army truck with other soldiers, and as we were riding along, I noticed a little girl standing behind a post. As we were passing by her, she stepped out from behind this post, and began to smile at me. I caught the glimpse of her dark eyes looking at me. So, I waved to her and she waved back. Her eyes were saying to me, "Take me with you." That memory somehow has connected itself to my Chris.

The general superintendent for the general contractor on the Rapid Transit job called Rich Murphy complaining about my disposition. One day Rich and Vern came to the job site in a very amicable way, and confronted me with the complaint. They asked that I attend a meeting with them in the general contractor's office to try and resolve the situation. The general contractor's representatives took the floor and stated to Vern and Rich that they appreciated my capabilities, but, it was of their opinion that I wasn't pushing the crews hard enough and that I wasn't completing certain areas on schedule. They said that my attitude toward them was one that appeared to be that I didn't give a damn. They went on to say that if my attitude didn't change, they would expect Vern to have me replaced.

My forte had always been to negotiate any situation intelligently. But of forbearance I had none at that time. I knew better, but I became very belligerent, and verbally bellicose, which proved their point, of course. I abruptly stormed out of their office.

About ten minutes later, Rich and Vern approached me. Vern said, "Chuck, it looks like they have won the battle." Vern told me he would get back with me later in the day. They left the job site, and I continued on with my duties. I was very upset. I couldn't believe what they had said about me.

That evening, I received a call from Vern. He told me that he was going to put Don Salzman on the job to serve as the superintendent. He said he would appreciate it if I would work under Don. He wanted me to deal only with the placing of the steel, and to let Don do all of the communicating with the general contractor. "

"Rich said all of your benefits will remain the same for you. Just let Don run the show." I saw the wisdom of his terms and felt grateful for his protecting me. I agreed to his terms and hung up the phone.

Yet, in the night, the more I thought about what was happening to me, the madder I got. The next morning on my way to work, I convinced myself that I wasn't going to let Don take over my job. When I arrived at the job site, Don was there awaiting my arrival. It wasn't that I had a grudge against Don, because he was just as qualified as I was to run the job. He was a great person and we had always gotten along. So, I said, "No Don, I am not going to turn this job over to you." Don being the smart person he was said very politely, "I understand where you are coming from, and I will just go back to the office."

Within the hour, Vern came driving up, madder than hell.

He yelled at me, and said, "Chuck what in the hell is wrong with you? Last night you agreed to work with Don on this job, and now you are acting like a fool. I thought you were a much smarter man than what you are displaying here. You leave me no choice; I have to fire you. Give me the credit cards, and the keys to your truck."

I yelled back, "No! You can't have the keys to the truck; I have no way of getting home." He then said that he would have someone drive me home. "No way!" I said stubbornly, "If you want the truck, you will have to come to my house to get it." I have always regretted this stupid stunt that I had pulled, even before I got home. O, what a dolt!

Mary Ann couldn't understand what had come over me, and at the time, I didn't have any answers for her or me. I parked the company truck in front of our house. It sat there three days before they came to pick it up. I wasn't at home when they picked it up. I was out looking for another job.

Mary Ann told me that when they drove off with the truck, Christina started crying, and saying, "Mommy somebody is taking Daddy's truck away." She didn't understand. How could she?

I was beginning to feel like a nonentity. Finding a job wasn't as easy as I thought it was going to be. The word was out about the person that I had become. No company would hire me. Withdrawal from everyone began to dominate my behavior, loneliness ensued. I rejected myself; all that I had been, become and in doing so, rejected others and in turn was rejected by them. This vicious cycle was set in motion and was hard to break. I was becoming the person that I had not wanted to become. I wanted to be Dr. Jeykll, but had become Mr. Hyde.

I checked in with the Ironworkers Union in San Francisco, # 377. Red Fenton and Wayne Welsh were very understanding of my situation. They supported me in finding work. However, it was only work, it wasn't anything that I would write home about. Red and Wayne were great business agents.

I was blaming everyone for Christina's illness, including, and especially the doctors that had used faulty x-ray equipment. I believed, and still do to this day, that if they hadn't x-rayed her as much as they did for her hip, she would be alive today. My marriage was beginning to crumble; I verbally abused Mary Ann, constantly. How she managed to hold up is beyond comprehension. Chris was very supportive of her mommy. She would really scold me when I yelled at her mommy.

She would say to me, "Would you please shut up, and leave my mommy alone." Chris was the only one that could bring me down off my high-horse. I had turned into real jerk!

The companies, even Murphy, were sympathetic with my situation, but as Vern said, business is business. We have to have people that can get the job done with or without any emotional problems.

One evening I received a call from Bill Peppin, who had been my supervisor at Bethlehem Steel. He told me that Steel Erectors had lots of work coming up. He said for me to give the owner, Don Roberts, a call. Steel Erectors was situated in Fresno, California. I called Don, and he asked that I drive to Fresno, so that we could become better aquatinted.

When I arrived at Steel Erectors office, Don's secretary greeted me. She said that Don was expecting me, and for me to go right into his office. She asked if I would care for a cup of coffee; I told her I would. Don welcomed me with open arms. He was a younger man. We began exchanging our previous experiences in life and in business. He acknowledged that he was aware of my daughter's battle with Leukemia, and that he and his wife had lost their five years old daughter to pneumonia. She died while he was holding her in his arms.

Don started his business with a partner. They had only been in business for about four years, before dissolving their partnership. His partner started up his own business, competing against Steel Erectors. However, they remained friends, even until this day.

Don had a field superintendent taking care of the San Francisco Bay area by the name of Don Jackson. Don J. was a very fine young man; I had the utmost respect for him. He was a very knowledgeable and caring young man. Don R. asked if I would mind going to work with Don J. on the Sequim building in San Francisco. The building was twenty-two stories high. Of course I said that I would. He said that he had another job about to start, the Embarcadero Center in San Francisco, and he would like for me to run it. It was a forty-five-story building.

I reported for work on the Sequin Building in San Francisco. From San Jose it was about a forty-five minute drive. Don J. assigned me to a certain area to work. I knew that I had to maintain my composure, so that I could efficiently perform my job.

I really wanted to perform well for both Don's. Mentally, I realized that this would be my last chance of survival. I tried staying busy, to avoid thinking of Christina's illness. After working for Don for a couple of months, I began to simmer down my hostile attitude toward my family. At the time, little did I realize that Mary Ann was the greatest comforter of my life. In addition to her continuing love, she quoted some words to me that gave me some insight and enabled me to grow:

"*Life and death decisions are certainly debatable. Empathy and sympathy are the roller coaster juggernauts that every person must deal with at some time in their lives. If children are taught from birth by responsible loving parents that choices are hard to make; if the wrong choice is made, a consequence follows. If a right choice is made our collective integrity is rewarded. (God, Parents, Schoolteachers, etc). The human debate of life or death can only be dealt with at the time of each instance. If we try to prepare ourselves for such a catastrophic occurrence, the catastrophe may be so different or devastating from our prepared thoughts that we are still left without a plan and must rely on collective integrity.*" I have always tried to have an open mind regarding Pneumatology. However, these words, coming from Mary Ann, compelled me to re-examine my life, my goals, and my expectations. Life is all I, or anyone for that matter, can have at any given moment. We have to play the hand we are dealt. We may win some hands or lose some, but ultimately we live and then die. The thought that so rankled my emotions was that for those we love, death may shorten the game. My emotions began to return to some normality but always there was the undercurrent of anger and sadness, but tinged with hope.

The Embarcadero Center was a very large project. It covered one square block. The footings went down 30 feet below ground level. Don put me on the job early to set up our job office, so that I could become familiar with the plans, and coordinate the steel deliveries with Bethlehem Steel. During the excavation, we found ruins dating back to 1906, which was the year of the great earthquake in San Francisco. An Apothecary, or whatever they were called in those days, had probably been standing somewhere in the vicinity of this block until the earthquake destroyed it. We found lots of empty medication bottles: some large and some small. I gathered up as many as I could. I kept them for several years, until they just disappeared in the course of moving.

I was finally and really mentally prepared for this job. I was bound and determined to do what no man has done before. From the size of this job, I envisioned we could place a minimum of four tons per man, in an eight-hour shift. The footing was five feet in depth, and consisted of four layers of Re-Bar. All were #11 (a number eleven bar is 1-1/4 inch in diameter, and weighs 5.313 pounds per lineal foot.) It makes for hard work.

The bottom layers of #11s were supported on a continuous poured-in-place concrete bar support, 3" off of the ground and were placed on 12" centering each way. The second layer was placed 2 ft. higher, and the third layer was placed another 2 ft. higher. The top layer was placed 2" from the top of the footing. All of these layers of Re-Bar were supported with templates of angle iron, L 6 x 4 x 7/8 weighting 27.2 lbs. per ft.

When I submitted my tonnage report, Don's secretary, Beverly, had stated that she had never heard of so much steel being placed in such a short time. She and Don were really impressed. Don was so impressed that he offered me the General Superintendent's job in the Los Angles area. The superintendent that he had in L.A. was to retire within two months.

This was one time when I was very reluctant about accepting Don's offer. This would mean that Mary Ann would be left all alone with Christina and the boys. Edward was a sophomore in High School and was doing very well on the Baseball team at James Lick High School. Baseball was his greatest love. If I took them out of school I would be doing the same thing that my dad did to me during my sophomore year of High School. I had always promised myself that I would never take my sons out of a school where they had established themselves, especially during their high school years. I felt that those years were the most important.

However, Don continued insisting that I accept his offer, because of the workload in L.A. It was getting very low, and he wanted me to bid on jobs with Bethlehem, and try to build up the workload. At the time, there was lots of work coming up for bid. We had to make a decision. Christina's medical bills were overwhelming. My insurance only covered 80% of her medical costs. If I accepted the transfer to the Los Angles area, we would be able to take Chris to the City of Hope in Duarte, California, and wouldn't have to pay anything above what my insurance covered.

It was the consensus of the family that I accept Don's offer. I assured Don that I would give it my best shot, but I wasn't sure if I was emotionally capable, due to Christina's illness. He assured me that he would work with me. Don told me on my way to Los Angeles that I was to stop by the office in Fresno and have Beverly give me enough cash to start off with in L.A.

During my journey to Los Angeles, I had this craven feeling that I might not be doing the right thing. The other times I had left home had been adventures for my entire family. There were times during my trip that day when I would nearly turn my truck around with the intention of not accepting this job. For God's sake, I would say, I am the father of my little sick beloved daughter and I should be taking care of her. Why am I leaving her and my family behind? This was the very nadir of my life. I was still, but less, angry, confused, torn apart by doubt in myself.

Before leaving San Jose, Christina said, "Daddy, be sure to call us when you get to Disneyland." I had promised her that when she and mommy came to visit me that we would take her to Disneyland, and Knott's Berry Farm. She was so ecstatic, she would say, "Oh, I can hardly wait." My heart was wrenched. Waiting is the one thing she could hardly do.

I didn't have a place in mind about where I would live when I arrived in Los Angles. All I could think about was that I needed to find a place near Disneyland. So when I entered the outskirts of L.A. I continued on driving towards Orange County. I drove all the way to Disneyland. And then I got back on the Santa Ana freeway, and headed back toward L.A. I hadn't been traveling more than ten minutes when I saw a sign that said Fullerton. I veered off to the right, and drove through this quaint town of Fullerton. I liked what I saw, so I began looking for an apartment to rent. I was driving down Bacon Street, when I saw an apartment complex, with a sign posted for rent. I stopped in and met the managers. There was a one bedroom available.

"However, we have not had time to clean it since the last renter moved out."

I said, "Well, I needed a place to stay for the night, so I will clean the apartment myself."

Okay, they said, we will deduct $50.00 off of your first month's rent. I agreed to rent the apartment on a month-to-month base. I had rented the apartment without even seeing it and, believe me, it was in a mess. I went to the store and bought some detergents, and started cleaning away. I began to have a greater appreciation of what Mary Ann had to go through on each move.

I went to J.C. Penny's to buy bedding, pillows and some cooking utensils. I didn't have anything. After completing my chores, I called Mary Ann from a pay phone. They were happy that I had arrived okay. Mary Ann began to cry, and said that she felt like she had been abandoned. Of course her statement didn't make me feel any better than how badly I was already feeling. I asked her if she would like me to give up on this job and return back to San Jose. She said, no you have already accepted it, so just stay. I did know that this move was very hard for her. I told her that as soon as the Phone Company hooked up my telephone, I would let her know what the number was.

The next day, I went by the Phone Company and requested that they put a phone in my apartment, in Steel Erectors name. That evening, they did so. When they completed the installation, I called Mary Ann, and the office to let them know what my number was.

Don said, "Just hang around and I'll be down tomorrow to introduce you to the group at Bethlehem Steel."

The next day, Don and his pilot arrived at the Fullerton Airport. Don owned his own plane. I met them at the airport, and we departed for Bethlehem's office building. When we arrived, he introduced me to the group. Some of them I had met before, when I worked for San Jose Steel in Grass Valley.

Oscar Haggard, who was a sales representative for Bethlehem, showed me where the plan room was. This would be the place where I would come to when I had to review the plans for bidding on any upcoming jobs. They would call me when the jobs became available.

When we left Bethlehem's office, we went to have lunch with Arnold Bacon, who was Don's Field Superintendent. Arnold was happy that I had come aboard, because he was ready for retirement. He brought me up to speed, regarding the manpower situation in the Los Angeles area. He gave me the names and phone numbers of his key foreman. I agreed to meet with Arnold the next day, so that he could show me the existing jobs that Steel was working on in the area. It would also give me a chance to meet the foremen.

I took Don and his pilot back to the airport, and they departed for Fresno. I immediately went back to my apartment, and called Mary Ann. She said, "Bernice and Ed have agreed to drive us to Disneyland this coming week-end." The hospital staff at Stanford told me that any child with cancer would be welcome at Disneyland, and Knott's Berry Farm at no charge. Parents and all guests would be admitted at no charge as well.

The next morning I called Disneyland, and Knott's Berry Farm to inquire about how to get tickets. They told me to come by their office and sign up, listing all of the names of my family and guests. They would also need the names of the doctors at Stanford, so they could call and verify Christina's condition. After I completed all of the necessary paper work, we could attend Disneyland and Knott's Berry Farm anytime we wanted to. And, believe me, we certainly did visit these places very often. My family and I will always be grateful for Disneyland and Knott's Berry Farm's kindness and consideration. May God bless Walt Disney and all of his staff for helping a little girl enjoy a part of her little life while here on earth. This is probably the only way we could reciprocate for your kindness.

With the exception of Edward, who stayed behind in San Jose, the family arrived in Fullerton. My apartment wasn't big enough for Ed, Bernice, and Bobby to stay with us, so they had to stay in a motel. Mary Ann, Arnold, and Chris stayed with me in the apartment. Arnold slept on the couch, and Chris slept with Mary Ann and me. They all were tired out from the trip. The next morning, Ed, Bernice, and Bobby came over to the apartment and we all left together for Disneyland. We decided that we would eat breakfast at Disneyland.

We didn't have any problems entering the gates at Disneyland. There were long lines waiting, but we went straight to the front and they greeted us with the utmost kindness. They told me when I had signed up that we wouldn't have to wait in any lines, and that included all rides, as well. We all enjoyed a delicious breakfast at the Mickey Mouse Pancake House.

Chris said, "The Mickey Mouse Waffle is my favorite."

Disneyland provided a stroller for Chris. It sure did come in handy, because there were times when she would become a little tired while walking. And she did love to walk around Disneyland. We took her on every ride that she wanted to go on, which was most of them. Her favorite ride was Small World.

Arnold and Bobby really enjoyed themselves as well. Bobby was 13, and Arnold was 12. They rode on every ride. We told them that they could have the run of Disneyland, but to be careful. We told them to be sure to meet us at a certain place, at a certain time, for lunch. They were very good boys. We ate lunch at the same place we had eaten breakfast. Chris wanted another Mickey Mouse Waffle. She loved all of the cherries and whipped cream on her waffle. Mary Ann, Ed, Bernice and I stayed with Chris, watching her enjoy all of the amusements. She really had a wonderful time. I told her that this was her day, and anything that she wanted she could have. She was our Queen for the Day.

We spent the entire day at Disneyland. By the end of the day we were all beginning to tire, so it was the consensus of the family that we leave and return to my apartment. When we arrived it was still a beautiful and warm day, so the boys wanted to go swimming in the pool. Ed and I had to take them to buy bathing suits. We decided, while we were out, that we would buy some Chinese food and bring it back to the apartment for dinner.

While we were out, Mary Ann, Bernice, and Chris sat out in the chairs around the pool. Mary Ann said that Chris would sit with her feet dangling in the warm water. After a while she had become a little sleepy, so Mary Ann laid her down on the bed to take a nap. When we arrived, Arnold and Bobby put their suits on, and dove into the pool. They both were good swimmers.

Before too long, Chris woke up, and said that she was hungry, so we all ate dinner. She really liked Chinese food. About ten o'clock that night, Ed, Bernice, and Bobby went back to their motel. We all knew that we had another big day ahead of us the next day. We would be going to Knott's Berry Farm.

The next morning, Ed, and family arrived and we left, going to Knott's Berry Farm. We were greeted with the same hospitality that we experienced at Disneyland. It seemed as if they couldn't do enough for us. A young girl, an employee of the park, took Christina's hand and walked with her to show her some pictures of Knott's Berry. Chris was so cheerful. She asked the girl if they served Mickey Mouse Waffles.

The girl said, "Yes we do. Are you hungry?"

Chris's was, "Yes! I'm about to starve to death."

The girl was dressed in a very colorful costume from the Pilgrims era. She was a great hostess. She asked if the rest of us were hungry, and of course we said we were. She escorted us to this fine open-air restaurant, and saw to it that we were seated at a table that was large enough for all of us. Our escort bid us farewell and bent down and hugged, and kissed Chris, and she said for her to enjoy herself at Knott's Berry. Chris said that she would, and thanked her.

We spent the entire day at Knott's Berry Farm. Chris and the boys really enjoyed themselves. At the end of the day we all were a bit fatigued, so we left and went back to my apartment. The boys got into their swimsuits and dove into the pool. They seem to have more energy than the rest of us. Chris was tired, and wanted to take a nap. While she was napping, we called in our order for Chinese food, and Ed and I went to pick it up. I knew that Chris would not be disappointed in having Chinese food two nights in a row. This was one of her favorite foods.

Ed wanted to adjourn early, because they were to leave the next morning for their trip back to San Jose. When they arrived at the apartment the next morning, Mary Ann had everything packed and ready to go. I loaded their belongings into Ed's car, and as usual we couldn't hold back a few tears. Chris said, "Daddy when we get back to San Jose, I will call you, and let you know that we had a safe trip. So, don't worry." How like her mother she was!

After they left, I went back into the apartment, and pulled out a bottle of bourbon, and poured myself a drink, chased with a seven up. I guess I was feeling sorry for myself. I began to cry and pray at the same time, asking God to spare Chris's life, and to let a cure become available for the dreadful disease that she had. I knew that there was no panacea for my darling little love. I cried and continued drinking until I fell asleep on the couch. This dreadful disease was not only affecting Chris's life, but it was affecting all of our lives. Deep down in my heart, I didn't really want this job. I wanted to be with my family, but I had no choice. I would have to suffer the consequences and stay on in southern California. That evening Chris did call, and she said, "Hi Daddy, well, we made it back home, safe and sound. I know that it is late, but I knew you would be worried, so I called you to let you know that we are okay." She and I had a nice long conversation; she expressed the good time she had at Disneyland and at Knott's. She also told me she couldn't wait until they moved to Fullerton. Then, she said, she could go to Disneyland every day. I said, "Yes, my love, that is our plan; we will take you there every day, I promise." Then she gave the phone to Mary Ann. Mary Ann told me how much they enjoyed their visit and how much it meant to be with me. She said they were pretty tired, so they were going to bed early. I told her that I would call them the next day.

The next day was Tuesday; I went to Arnold Bacon's house

to pick up some office equipment, and all the data pertaining to Steel's affairs. I then made the rounds of the three jobs that Steel had in progress. I knew that I was going to have to get more work for Don if we were to remain in Los Angles area. Don and I conversed every day. This one day I received a call from Ron Blackstock, who was the head sales person for Bethlehem. He said that they had 5 jobs in the plan room, and requested that I come in to review and bid on them. All of the jobs were either bridges or overpasses. There were other placers for Bethlehem who were also invited to bid on these jobs.

Every Friday, Beverly, Don's secretary, would call to tell me what flight to be on at LAX. She always saw to it that I got back to San Jose for my weekend stay with my family. Mary Ann and Chris would always meet me at the airport in San Jose. When I got off of the plane, I would go to the waiting room where they would be, and Chris would always come running toward me. We would always go through our usual routine of hugging and kissing. She would then ask me what I had for her as a surprise. And of course I would have a stuffed animal of some kind for her.

Since I always returned on Friday evening, we would go out for dinner with Ed, Bernice, and Bobby. Edward and Arnold went with us as well. But, before long, Edward started to feel like he was getting too big to go out with us and the other kids. But under these circumstances he would go with us. For dessert, on our way back home, we would stop by Winchell's and buy a dozen doughnuts. We would eat them, and have a joyful evening.

Mary Ann complained that our Plymouth Fury Station Wagon was too hard for her to drive, and it was too long to park in some of the parking lots that she had to park in, while taking Chris to Stanford. So Saturday morning, we took a drive to downtown San Jose and stopped at a Buick dealership. We traded the station wagon in for a beautiful 1969 Buick Riviera. It was fully equipped: all leather seats, air conditioning, spoke wheels with white side wall tires. We both really loved that car.

Mary Ann's, Mom, Helen, would be arriving from Seattle,

and would be staying with her for two weeks. Mary Ann and I decided that it was time for her and the kids to make the move to Fullerton. Helen would take care of Chris for a couple of days, while Mary Ann was in Fullerton with me, looking for a house to rent.

When Helen arrived, Mary Ann called me to let me know what time she would be arriving at the L.A. airport. Chris said, "It will be okay for mommy to leave her with Nanny and fly to meet Daddy, so we can all move to Disneyland." She told mommy not to worry about her, because she and Nanny would be just fine. And she finished with the flourish that Aunt Bee would be there as well.

I met Mary Ann at the airport, and we visited with about three real estate companies in Fullerton. One agent had a listing in a very elite section of Fullerton, called Sunny Hills. This house was located at 2246 Via Ingreso, Fullerton. He showed us the house, and we both knew that this was the one. It was a two-story house, with four bedrooms, and a beautiful view of Disneyland. We knew that Chris would really love this house. The owner was a beautiful young girl who was the girl friend of Jimmy Dean, the country singer, who owned Jimmy Dean's Sausage. We signed a 12-month lease agreement, and paid the first and last month rent in advance. Mary Ann spent the night with me, and the next day I took her back to the airport, and she departed for San Jose. She didn't want to be away from Chris too long.

I informed Don of our intentions, and told him that I would have to take off work for at least a week to get moved and settle in our new house. He said, "No problem." I called Mary Ann to tell her that I would be renting a U-Haul truck, and that one of our employees would be coming with me to help load and unload our furniture. His name was Gary Smith. He was one of our welders. He was the best, bar none.

When Gary and I arrived, Mary Ann and Helen had everything packed, ready to go. Edward and Arnold assisted Gary and me with the loading of our furniture, which wasn't much, because we didn't have very much. After we finished with the loading of the truck, we hit the road for Fullerton. Before leaving, Ed, Bernice, and Bobby came over to say by to us. Helen stayed with Bernice for the remainder of her visit.

During our trip to Fullerton, we stopped at a motel with the kids, for the night. Gary didn't want to stop over for the night, so he drove the U-Haul straight through to Fullerton without stopping, except for gas and coffee. I gave him a key to our house in the event he wanted to start unloading some of the small things into the house. The next day when we arrived, Gary was waiting for us at the house. He had already off loaded some of the smaller things into the house. The boys and I helped him off load the rest of the furniture. He then left and went back to his home in the San Fernando Valley.

This move was in September of 1969. We settled into our rented house and tried to carry on with life the best we could. Edward and Arnold entered school in Sunny Hills. It took some adjusting for them. I continued on with my work, which was very difficult. I just wasn't able to concentrate. My mind kept turning to Christina and her illness all day long. I knew that one day I would come home from work, and she wouldn't be there to greet me. As it was, when I came home, I would hug and kiss her, and look into her beautiful brown eyes, and try to avoid crying. I would get all choked up. I just couldn't imagine what we would do without her. I was doing everything in my power to see that she lived.

Mary Ann and I drove over to the City of Hope to check Chris in. It was a real nice place. We met Christina's Doctor. His name was Dr. Rosenberg. We found him to be a wonderful man. He showed compassion for the parents as well as for his patients. Chris was the primary patient, but so were all her family to Dr. Rosenberg. Chris would always refer to him as "her guy." She really was taken with him. Mary Ann would drive to the City of Hope on an average of three times per week. Dr. Rosenberg wanted to keep close tabs on her blood count on a bi-weekly basis.

Edward seemed to fit in very well with the kids at Sunny Hill High. Arnold seemed to have some real smart mouth teachers. One of them I will define later on. One thing for sure, when Mary Ann didn't have to take Chris into the hospital, we would either be at Disneyland or Knott's Berry. We never had to spend one dime at either one of those places.

We had been awarded several jobs through Bethlehem Steel. Our work force was overwhelming. There just weren't enough rodmen to go around. Work was that plentiful. Bruce 'Duke' Parkhurst was the Business Manager for Local Union # 416. He supported me in every way that he possibly could. He said that if I wanted to hire anybody, for me to just send him or her in and he would see to it that they were dispatched out to Steel. They don't come any better than the 'Duke.'

I hadn't expected all of the work that we were awarded, nor had I anticipated such a manpower shortage. I spent 90% of my time on the phone and in my truck traveling. My truck was equipped with phone and radio. In the heat of summer, I would receive calls from irate contractors, wanting more manpower. My phone at home was always ringing off of the hook, into the late hours of the night.

Christina's health was continuing to fail. From January of 1970, she would spend 90% of her life in the hospital at the City of Hope. It was a very difficult time for the family. Edward and Arnold were practically taking care of themselves, and Mary Ann was spending just about all of her time at the hospital with Chris. I was there with them as much as I could be. I had to attend meetings with various contractors. I never had a free moment to spend with Chris. I was in and out of the hospital everyday for very brief stints.

Every morning, before making my job rounds, I would stop at the hospital to see how my baby was doing. One morning, I went into her room, and she wasn't there. I started looking around and found her walking down the hall. Suddenly, I head a nurse scream at her, "Christina, go back to your room, and get in the bed, and I mean now." Chris yelled back at her, "I don't want to, and you can't make me." Chris then saw me, and came running toward me. I picked her up, and asked her, "Honey what's the matter?" She said, "That nurse was mean to her, and had been all morning long." The nurse then saw me, and said, "Christina needs to learn some manners."

I screamed at that nurse and said, "Damn it, she is not in here to learn manners, and don't you ever let me hear you scream at her again. If you don't like your job, I will help you get relieved of it." I reported her actions to Dr. Rosenberg, and from that day forward, she and Chris were the best of friends. I don't know what Doc said, but she couldn't do enough for Chris, Mary Ann, or me.

One evening after completing my daily activities, I stopped by the hospital to visit with Chris and Mary Ann. I'd had a very hectic day, and was not in the very best of moods. Mary Ann said something to me that really ticked me off, and through my own ignorance, I blatantly yelled at her. Chris came to Mary Ann's defense, and said, "Daddy you get out of here, and leave my mommy alone."

Realizing that what I had said was wrong, I apologized, and promised her that I wouldn't do it again. I left earlier than usual. Life was taking its toll with me. I cried all the way home. This other person that I had become, I didn't like. It didn't matter what Mary Ann would say to me, I became angry. We were cross with one another all the time. At least, I was cross with her and she'd respond in like manner. We were tight, tense, worried.

When I arrived at home, Edward and Arnold had taken lots of phone messages for me. I was getting to the point, where I wanted to tell everyone to take this job and shove it. I was under a tremendous amount of stress. Edward and Arnold were a great comfort to me during this terrible ordeal. Mary Ann had arrived, and again I apologized to her for my actions at the hospital in front of Chris.

She said, "I understand. I told Chris that Daddy loved her very much."

The next morning when I arrived at the hospital, I went directly to Chris's room. She lay awake, and before I could say anything, she said," Daddy I am sorry." I put my arms around her and kissed her. I was all choked up, I said, "Oh my darling, you don't have to apologize to Daddy. I am the one who is sorry, and I apologize to you, and I promise you that I will never yell at mommy again." She said, "Good." Shades or mom, I felt the doubt.

Soon Mary Ann arrived while I was still at the hospital, and we tried to display as many happy gestures as possible in Chris's presence. While we were joking around with Chris, two nurses entered, rolling a gurney with a 12-year old girl on it. The girl's hair was beginning to fall out, so we knew what was wrong with her. I had to leave, so I hugged and kissed Mary Ann and Chris goodbye.

That evening when I arrived back at the hospital, the parents of the 12-year-old girl were there with her. Mary Ann and the parents had become pretty well aquatinted during the day. They were from Fresno. Their daughter had been transferred to the City of Hope. The reason for them being there was the same reason as ours, which was the lack of enough insurance. The two of them were pretty much devastated over their daughter's illness.

"The doctors in Fresno had told us that our daughter didn't have long to live." He said.

City of Hope provided them a room where they could stay during the time their daughter was there. We got to know them pretty well over a two week period. Their daughter died about ten days after she arrived. If people could only see what children and parents go through during these deadly times, I think, maybe they might think twice before abusing a child in any way. Of course there are people that care less about the life of a child than they do of their own selfishness. Those kinds of people don't deserve to live on this earth. (This is politically incorrect, but, I believe it!)

We weren't truthful with Chris when she asked where her friend had gone. What does a parent say or do in a situation like that? We said that her mommy and daddy had to take her back home to Fresno. I said they would write to us. (We did receive a Christmas card from them the following year).

The nurse requested that I be at the hospital the next day to help them draw some of Chris's bone marrow. I was there, but my God, what a terrible ordeal Mary Ann and I had to go through. Chris was carted into another room, and they asked that I hold her down on her side while they withdrew her bone marrow. The pain was so excruciating for her. She looked me in the eye, and began screaming, saying, "Daddy what are they doing to me?"

She cried so hard that red dots popped out all over her little body. I kept yelling at the nurse, how much longer, for God's sake. The nurse would say, "Not much longer."

Bless her heart; afterwards Chris was so weak and tired. Mary Ann and I were so full of sorrow and pain for our baby, but there was nothing we could do. My God, my God!

When they finished this terrible ordeal, they rolled her back into her room. Chris was clinging to Mary Ann all the way, and even in her room, she wouldn't let go of her mommy. The red dots were still on her little body.

The stress from my job began taking its toll, and coupled with Chris's ordeal, I wasn't able to function properly. I asked Don to relieve me from my job, because of my dysphoria. I just wasn't able to carry on under such stress. He said, Hang in there. It would all be over soon." I wasn't sure if he meant Chris' life or the job.

Mary Ann and I spent the rest of the day with Chris. Later on in the day, the red spots on Chris's little body began to fade away: and her color began to show signs of a normal child. Her skin was a milky white during this terrible ordeal. She told Mary Ann that she was hungry. Mary Ann instructed the nurse to have some food sent in for Chris.

It had been a long and emotional day for the three of us. So Mary Ann told Chris that we would be leaving and that we would return early tomorrow morning. Chris always seemed to understand when her mommy told her something. She would never rebel, or say; no I don't want you to leave. Some of the kids that were in the hospital would scream when their parents left them for the evening. Mary Ann and I hugged and kissed Chris as we were leaving. We could hear her sweet little voice drift down the hall as we were walking away, repeatedly saying, "I love you mommy, I love you daddy, see you tomorrow."

Mary Ann would yell back, "We love you too honey, see you tomorrow." This was more difficult than combat.

It was all we could do to hold back our tears. We were so choked up we couldn't say a word to one another before leaving the hospital. Mary Ann got into her car, I got into my truck, and we left for home. We held each other for a while and got into bed.

The next morning I arrived at the hospital very early. When I entered Chris's room, she was wide awake, smiling and saying, "Good morning Daddy. I have a new friend with me today. Her name is Ann."

I hugged and kissed Chris as I always do, and I told her that I was glad to meet her little friend.

Ann was a four-year old African American child. She had Sickle Cell Anemia Disorder. Sickle Cell Disease is a condition confined almost exclusively to black Africans and African-Americans. A few minutes later, Ann's mom and dad entered the room. I introduced myself, and they introduced themselves. They said that Ann had just recently been diagnosed with her disorder. They were both clearly devastated. The father's name was Ben, and the mother's name was Rachel. Ann was their only child. Rachel wasn't too coherent. She was all choked up as she was hugging and kissing Ann. Ben bent over her bed and kissed her.

He asked her. "How is my little girl feeling?"

Ann said, "Fine Daddy."

Mary Ann arrived about 30 minutes later and I introduced her to Ann, Rachel, and Ben. Over the next week, we got to know them pretty well. Ben was a Professor at Santa Clara College, and Rachel was a fifth grade school teacher in Santa Clara, California. In those days there was still a certain amount of prejudice between blacks and whites. However, I learned an awful lot from these two wonderful people. One thing I learned was: it wasn't the color of ones skin that characterizes ones charisma; it is what is within ones heart that describes God's everlasting love. Their acquaintance opened up a wide range of perspectives in my life. I realized that there was no color barrier between us. Ben and Rachel loved their child as much as Mary Ann and I loved ours. I will never forget their friendship.

One morning when I arrived at the hospital, I went into Chris's room, and she had a sad look on her face, and I asked, "What was the matter darling?" Chris said, "Ann had to be put into another room last night, because she had become sick."

I tried to comfort her as much as I could. Chris said to me, "Daddy how much longer will I have to stay here in the hospital, I want to go home and see Nikie (our dog) and swing on my swing." I told her, "It will not be much longer honey. Maybe you can go home tomorrow or the next day. We will have to hear what the doctor thinks."

The night before when they took Ann out of Chris's room, it was because she had died. I didn't know this until the nurse informed me later. We never saw or heard from Ben or Rachel after that, but our hearts went out to them. Someday, we would have to face what these other loving parents were undergoing right now.

When Mary Ann arrived at the hospital, I informed her of Ann's dying, and she said, "Oh no! "She could detect that Chris was feeling sad over her little friend being taken out of her room. Chris said, "Now I won't have anybody to talk to." Mary Ann said to her, "Oh, yes you will honey. Mommy will stay here with you. I had to leave to attend another meeting with Bethlehem Steel regarding a steel strike. How I wished I could have stayed there.

It was a long and tiring day attending this stupid meeting. I was sure glad when we adjourned. I called Mary Ann at the hospital to see how Chris was doing, and she said, "She

is doing fine." I told her that I wasn't feeling too well, and that I would be going home to rest. She told me that would be fine, and that she would be home as soon as Chris went to sleep.

I went home and met with Edward and Arnold, and we went out for dinner. I could tell that the effects of Chris's illness were taking its toll on them, too. They both asked the question, "How much longer did she have to live?" I said that I didn't know and that we would just have to keep praying for a miracle. We finished dinner, and went back to the house. I went to bed early, I was pretty well exhausted. As I was lying in the bed sound asleep, I heard Mary Ann's voice saying, "Daddy wake up, and look whose here."

I did awake, and it was a miracle. Mary Ann had brought Chris home for the weekend. I said, thank God, and I reached out to Chris with open arms. We embraced. I could hardly hold back the tears. I was really choked up. I told Mary Ann that I would sleep on the couch downstairs, and she and Chris could sleep in our bed. I knew they would rest better without me rolling around as I always do.

The next morning, I just did not report for work. I stayed home with Chris and Mary Ann. Chris was very happy to be home with Nikie and the boys. Chris had begun to lose her hair, and she didn't understand why. But she never complained. She was also on Prednisone. Prednisone and Prednisolone are entirely comparable regarding potency, therapeutic efficacy and side effects. Their anti-inflammatory and antiallergenic actions are approximately five times as powerful, but their salt-retaining effect is less pronounced than that of cortisone. Her little body was puffy, especially her face. We had a little plastic pool in the back yard for her but when she wanted to go out and splash around, she said, "Daddy, you know, I may have to go on a diet; because my swimming suit is a little tight." Bless her heart. It may be that in some ignorance there is bliss.

My phone kept ringing off of the hook every 5 minutes with contractors wanting to know why I hadn't showed up on some of their jobs. I tried to explain to them why I wasn't working this day. Some of them were sympathetic and some of them were real assholes.

We tried to make Chris's stay at home as comfortable as we could. She wanted me to go to McDonald's and get some French fries and a big chocolate milk shake. I did, and when I returned with her order, she was playing in the back yard with Nikie. She would throw a tennis ball, and he would chase after it. She really laughed at him. Mary Ann was sitting in a lawn chair, watching after her. She had to make sure that Chris didn't fall and injure herself.

Edward had worked for me in the summer of 1969, and he had saved up enough money to buy himself a Honda motorcycle. So I had to buy Arnold a Honda dirt bike. Chris wanted me to give her a ride on Arnold's bike. So I placed her on the seat in front of me, and we took a tour of the neighborhood. When we returned to the house, she look down at her right leg and saw that she had a burn from the exhaust pipe of Arnold's bike. Apparently she didn't feel any pain from it; she was mostly concerned about the redness from it.

She became very angry with me, and said, "Daddy, why did you let me get burned? I am going to tell mommy on you." I felt terrible about my lack of attention and scared that she had not felt the burning. I was helpless.

Our weekend with Chris was very pleasant. However, on Monday morning, Chris was feeling very ill. Mary Ann called the hospital and they told us to bring Chris back to the hospital.

Chris' condition was getting worse. I called Bernice in San Jose to inform her of Chris's condition, and she said that she, Ed, and Bobby would drive down the coming weekend Bernice, Ed, and Bobby arrived around 6 p.m., Friday evening. Chris was elated to see her Aunt Bee.

Ed, Bernice, and Bobby spent the night at our house. The next morning, Edward, Arnold, Ed, Bernice, and Bobby followed Mary Ann and me over to the hospital to be with Chris. When we arrived, Chris was glad to see us, but we could tell that she wasn't feeling very well. Ed, and the boys and I went down to the hospital cafeteria to eat breakfast. When we finished, we returned to Chris's room. Mary Ann and Bernice left to go and eat. When they returned, the nurse helped us put Chris into a wheel chair so we could roll her outside to enjoy some of the sunshine. She had to have an IV attached to the wheel chair. We could tell from the expression on Chris's face that she wasn't feeling well. Bernice took quite a few pictures of her.

Chris said, "I would like to go back to my room, because I feel dizzy, kinda funny."

So we rolled her back into her room and I gently picked her up and put her back into her bed. Mary Ann called for the nurse to come in to check on Chris. The nurse said, "You should all leave her alone for a while, because Chris needs rest." She said she was going to give her a sleeping pill to make her sleep. Mary Ann and Bernice stayed with Chris during the whole time she was asleep. Bernice and Ed decided they just had to go back to San Jose that evening, because Ed had to be at work on Monday morning. We really did appreciate them coming to see Chris. It was a long drive for them.

It is not easy for me to write about these personal memories of this time, about my little angel and my family's suffering. We began to sense the slowly approaching 11th hour and were filled with impending dread. My family and I had no one to turn to for counseling. So, finally I did call Pastor Andre Bustanoby at the First Baptist church in Fullerton, and asked him if he would come to the hospital and speak with us. He said that he would. The next day he arrived, and was very helpful in making the arrangements for the inevitable. He prayed with us, and for us. He asked God to open up the gates of Heaven so that Chris could return to Him as an Angel of God. He asked Him to be with us in our grief as we mourned the loss of our beloved child.

Before Pastor Bustanoby left to go back to his Church in Fullerton, he assured us that everything was in God's hands and for us not to worry. He said he would take care of all of the necessary arrangements.

On March 6, I received a call from Don Roberts instructing me to call the men to inform them that he was going out of business. He said he didn't want them to show up for work. He told me he had to file for bankruptcy. This decision really created turmoil within Bethlehem Steel and the Ironworkers Union. The fallout from this took lots of my time away from being with Chris in her last days here on earth with us.

My own personal feeling regarding Don's situation was that he should have called Bethlehem Steel to inform them of his intentions first. Because they were the ones that he was under contract with, but he left this all up to me. John Aston, (head of Bethlehem's detailing dept.) tried to get me to stay on, and to keep the men on the jobs that Steel Erectors were under contract to complete. He assured me of a much brighter future if I would accept his offer. But I decided to stick it out with Don, and in doing so, destroyed my credibility to some extent. But, I felt like that I owed Don this much, because I hadn't been able to perform as I should have, given my circumstances. I hated this situation for Don's sake, but I felt somewhat relieved that I had retained my own sense of integrity.

Clare Aston, who was the general field superintendent for Southwest Steel Rolling Mills called me as soon as he had heard that Global was no longer in business, and offered me the job position of general foreman over the Balboa Water Treatment Plant in the San Fernando Valley. I met with Clare and accepted his offer. It was a huge job; over 15,000 tons of reinforcing steel. Peter Kiwit & Sons was the general contractor. I could hardly even think about it, but decided to air it with Mary Ann.

Chapter 11

On April 8, 1970, Edward and Arnold were with us at the hospital. Mary Ann and I were very angry with one another. I don't have an explanation as to why I was such a jerk toward Mary Ann. I knew that there was nothing that either one of us could do to save our daughter's life. I couldn't understand why God had sent Chris to us, and then taken her away at such an early age. I prayed hard, but it didn't seem to matter. The old question about why God let innocent children suffer was beyond me.

Doctor Rosenberg requested a consultation with us. He said, "Chris's condition has worsened, and that he didn't expect her to live out the night." He continued, "I will order a shot of morphine. It will keep her sedated until the end."

Chris was under an oxygen tent, and having a difficult time breathing. She had asked that I go and get Nikie and bring him around to the window so that she could see him. We had brought Nikie with us that day. I went to the car and got him, and brought him to the window of Chris's room. When she saw Nikie, she smiled. I then took him back to the car. When I got back into Chris's room, she said that he was such a cute little dog.

Edward and Arnold were in the waiting room. I went to their side to try and comfort them as best I knew how. Their faces were drawn. They knew that God was about to take their precious little sister away from them and they knew that there was nothing they could do to prevent it from happening. Their helplessness echoed mine—like father, like sons.

I went back into Chris's room and observed that she was

deteriorating very rapidly. Mary Ann was kneeling down beside her and praying. I heard her say, "Oh, Jesus, please don't let Chris suffer. If it be your will, please take her now."

Chris began bleeding internally. Mary Ann was trying to remove clots of blood from her mouth. I reached in under the oxygen tent and removed the clots for her. The odor from the dried blood clots was terrible. It was all that I could do to keep from throwing up. Mary Ann and I were together in Chris' room but in our own private hells. Mary Ann was sitting in the chair beside her and I was standing over Chris at the other side of the bed near the window. Mary Ann whispered in a broken voice to "close the curtains because the sun is shining on Chris' face." I stepped over to the window. Outside lots of Humming Birds were buzzing around the window. So much energy there! I closed the curtains and returned to Chris's side. She turned her head slowly and looked at me as if to say thank you Daddy. She rolled her little head over to the right looking at her mother and closed her eyes. At 5:03 p.m. on Wednesday, April 8, 1970 our baby died of Leukemia at the City of Hope Hospital in Duarte, California.

I choked out to Mary Ann, "She's gone!"

Mary Ann calmly removed the oxygen tent and picked Chris up. She swayed back and forth, our daughter in her arms, and said to her, "Honey, you left us the same time that you were given to us , 5:03 p.m." A great silence seemed to enfold us in that room.

I went out to the waiting room to inform Edward and Arnold of Chris' dying. They began to snuffle and then to cry openly. We went together into Chris's room. Mary Ann had placed Chris back on the bed. Edward bent down and kissed her good-bye. They both were full of sadness. Mary Ann picked Chris's little body up and handed her to Arnold, "Hold on to her Arnold, because this is the only way you will remember her." Doctor Rosenberg and a nurse were standing by. I could read the sadness and frustration in their faces. They had done their best and like us, lost.

When Chris died, a part of all of us died. We sat a while in the silence. The nurse said that it would be best if they took her body down to morgue, so that they could wrap it, and send it to the mortuary. I asked her to not let the mortician twist her little arms while they were wrapping her little body.

Mary Ann and I took Edward and Arnold back home. Then Mary Ann and I went downtown to Backs-Kaulbars Mortuary in Anaheim to make arrangement for Chris's funeral. We selected the casket, and wrote them a check for their services. We went with the driver of the hearse to the hospital to pick up Chris's body. They rolled her little body out and placed it inside of the hearse. She was wrapped like a mummy from head to toe with a solid white covering. On our way back, we kept looking in the back of the hearse to see if Chris was alive. Of course we knew she had died, but hope springs eternal. Mary Ann and I were filled with anger. We were probably blaming each other for her death. We did not speak a word on the way back to the mortuary. Then, there were no words I had to comfort me, let alone to comfort Mary Ann; nor had she any. Chris had been ill for two and a half years before she died. Words were inadequate. Anger and grief overran our hearts and minds.

We left the mortuary and returned home. We were still not speaking to one another. I had called Pastor Bustanoby informing him of where Chris's body was and that we were planning on having her funeral service at Cryptside, Loma Vista Mausoleum, On April 11, at 10: a.m. He assured me that he would perform the service for Chris and us.

Mary Ann called all of our in-laws to inform them of Chris's death. Ed, Bernice, and Bobby from San Jose came. Margaret and her son Biff came down from Seattle. Helen also came from Seattle. My Mother, Dad, and Brother joined us from Alabama. We received Sympathy cards and flowers from all over. The one that touched me the most was the flower arrangement that her little friends in San Jose had sent.

I became very withdrawn. I didn't want any of our in-laws to attend Chris's funeral. I did not want to share our loss with anyone except Mary Ann, Edward, and Arnold. I was in a state of frustrated stasis. I became rebellious toward my friends, my wife and sons, and God. I was not about to forgive anyone for taking my baby away from me. My cries came from the very core of despair, of my desolation. My rebellious attitude toward my in-laws was warrantable. Why should I have to share my grief with them, when all of the years that she was sick, my parents' only came to see her twice? Margaret never came down from Seattle to see her. I convinced myself that the only reason she did come to the funeral was so that she could stop in Reno on her way back home to Seattle. Bernice, Ed, Bobby, and Helen deserved to be at our side, because they shared Chris's and our suffering while she struggled for life. Even before we put Chris to rest, my brother had wanted me to drive him to Oxnard to visit a friend of his. My parents, I felt, could have come to visit more often than they did, over the years. These were years that Mary Ann, Edward, Arnold and I needed comforting. Years later I became aware of how selfish I had become. Agony had been the center of my universe. I wanted it to be theirs too.

Even with all of our in-laws at our house, to some extent I ignored them. I went to the mortuary where Chris's body lay. I approached her little body lying in her white coffin. I spoke to her as if she were still alive. It almost seemed as if she were talking back to me. Her little hands were folded on her chest. She was dressed in a beautiful white dress. I touched her little hands, and rubbed her face with a gentle stroke. I then began to cry, praying at the same time. I was asking God, why? In reality, I was accusing God.

Later on in the morning, the rest of the family came to the mortuary to view Chris's body. My brother and Ed stepped up the coffin to view her body, and then they stepped back and became jocular. Mary Ann asked them to quit joking around and show respect. They bowed their heads in sorrow. This was a time in our lives when we weren't in the mood for laughter.

Pastor Bustanoby came in to express his sorrow, and to say a prayer over her body. He said that he would be at Loma Vista Mausoleum tomorrow morning.

The next day, April 11, 1970, was my Dad's Birthday. Everyone got dressed and went to the mortuary to follow the hearse to Loma Vista for the funeral services. Mary Ann and I were the last to leave. I had gotten dressed and was standing in our den looking at some of Chris' toys. I broke down and began to cry. Mary Ann came in and comforted me by putting her arm around me. She could see that I was having a hard time because I knew that this day would be the last time we would ever see our baby's body again.

When it was time to leave the mortuary, the funeral director organized everyone into his or her proper order of cars. Our car with Mary Ann, Edward, Arnold, and me, would follow directly behind the hearse to Loma Vista Mausoleum. Behind the hearse, not one of us spoke a word. We were immersed in our private wells of desolation, anger and loss. All I could see was the back of the hearse going down Harbor Boulevard that was lined with Palm trees, from Anaheim to Fullerton. A motorcycle cop escorted us. He would ride ahead, stopping all incoming traffic. We could see the people standing at the red lights, a few older men tipped their hats, watching as the hearse drove by.

We arrived at Loma Vista, where the director of the Mausoleum greeted us. We were all asked to wait in our cars while the caretakers were unloading Chris's coffin, so that they could arrange it for the funeral service. We had chosen a vault to place Chris's body in, because Mary Ann said that Chris's didn't like anything under ground.

When they were ready for us, Pastor Bustanoby came out to our car and walked with us, holding his Bible in his hand. He was trying to comfort us as much as possible. We entered the Mausoleum, were escorted to our seats directly in front of Chris's open casket.

Pastor Bustanoby opened the service with the benediction. He asked that everyone line up and walk past the coffin to pay their last respects. When everyone had moved past, the Pastor asked that all the other guests step outside the Mausoleum so that Mary Ann, Edward, Arnold and I could be with her alone, one last time. Mary Ann, Edward, and Arnold knelt at her coffin saying a silent prayer. Each of them kissed her good-bye.

I remained alone with her a few moments longer. I bent down over her coffin, promising her that sometime in the future we would be re-united. I touched and kissed her lovely face.

Everyone returned inside of the Mausoleum to view the cemetery workers closing the lid of the coffin. They rolled it down the hall and gently placed it in the vault. Her vault was the third one up from the bottom, at about 15 feet high. I looked back as we paraded out and threw her a kiss, like I always did when I would leave for work. On the front of her vault, we engraved, "Christina Margaret Herring, Our Little Love."

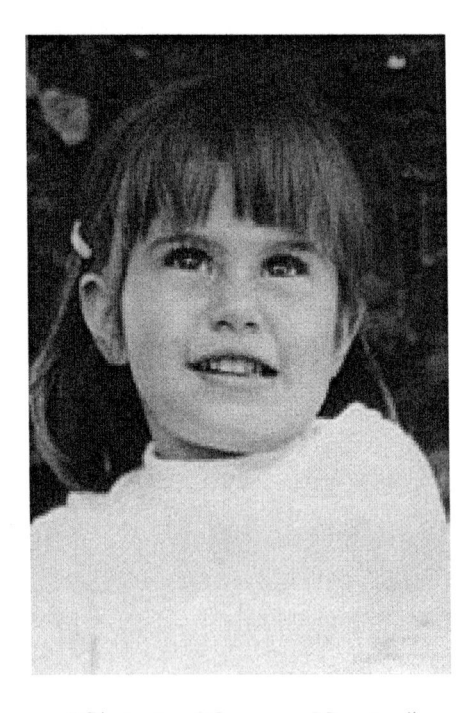

"Christina Margaret Herring"
Died from Leukemia
August 3, 1965 — April 8, 1970

Chapter 12

SURVIVAL

The kind of survival that one endures after losing a parent or friend, is nothing compared to losing a child at such an early age. Even though we grieve from the loss of our parents and friends, we seem to be able to accept and to live with and maintain our work-a-day lives after a period of time.

Arnold had a teacher who had given him a hard time from the first day he enrolled in school. The day after the funeral, she called me to report that my son Arnold had not attended school for the past week. I said that it was because of his little sister had died. She remained silent for a moment, and said, "I am sorry." And hung up the phone.

One "so called" charity read in the obituary column and noticed the listing of Chris's death. They called me to ask for a donation to the Leukemia Society. I was willing to donate. They left a phone number and an address for me to send my contribution. The next day I called the number they had given me, and there were no such number available. I called the better business bureau, and they said yes there was a rip off outfit out there working on the sympathy of the people who had recently lost a loved one from Leukemia. I came to realize that there was a whole world of people out there who never knew our Chris nor that she had died. There were also those ghoulish predators who will strike when one is most vulnerable.

After all of our family mourners had returned home, we tried to get on with life as best we could. Walking through the house and seeing Chris's toys was not easy. Edward and Arnold went back to school. I went back to work. Mary Ann would stay at home and try to comfort the three of us when we got home. Every morning before going to work, I would stop by the Mausoleum to visit Chris's Crypt, and say a little prayer. I would always throw her a kiss as I left. For the next eight years, night and day, seven days per week, I would stop in to visit with her. It comforted me.

I visited with every Church in Orange County, trying to seek the answer to why Chris had died. They all said, "First you will have to accept Jesus Christ as your savior, and tithe at least 10% of your earnings toward God's will, which you will donate to the Church." I wasn't ready to accept their answers or their divine accountancy terms. I did believe in God and a spiritual dimension but had trouble reconciling what they preached with what I felt.

Our marriage was beginning to crumble more so than ever. My frustrations continued and my verbal abuse toward my family continued, especially toward Mary Ann. I was not a happy person. I did not like what I had become. I was so grief stricken, I just wanted to die. We didn't have anyone to turn to for counseling, and I was getting angry. I would often go into a rage of violent outbursts, losing control. I wanted to punish whoever was responsible for Chris's death and that seemed to be everyone, myself included.

We tried going to the First Baptist Church in Fullerton, to express our sorrows to Pastor Bustanoby. However, his credibility slowly faded away, because he had become involved in a scandal, and the church had asked him to resign. I tried for sometime to keep up with his movements, but I soon lost track of him.

I continued working at the Balboa Water Treatment Plant, as described earlier. Peter Kiewit Sons were the General Contractor. All of their staff were sympathetic to our loss, especially Bob Davick and Jerry Toll. They commented several times that they thought that I was the best ironworker supervisor that they had ever worked with. As a matter of fact, after the Baloba Water Treatment Plant had been completed, I received a letter from Peter Kiewit, offering me a job on a large project that they had received the bid on just north of Great Falls, Montana. I was all prepared to accept their offer, when I received another letter from them stating that the job had been cancelled by the Government.

One warm, sunny afternoon, Mary Ann and I were riding around the neighborhood when we came upon a house that was for sale. It wasn't too far from where we were living. We called the listing agent to show us the house. When she arrived, we were waiting for her. The owner was a retired Lieutenant Colonel. The house was a two-story, 5 bedroom house. We really did like it, so I made an offer. That night at midnight we received a call from the agent, congratulating us, saying that we had bought a house.

I didn't have enough money on hand to make a down payment. I didn't think for a minute the owner would accept my low offer, but he did. So I had to get busy and come up with the money. My offer was that I would assume his equity of $10,000, and continue to make his house payments. He had purchased the house on his GI Bill at 5% interest. I had to rob Paul to pay Earl, but it was well worth it. This home became a haven from which we rebuilt our lives and love.

After we moved in Mary Ann and I decided that we should start back to school. She had been encouraged by the medical staff at the City of Hope to finish her education and become a Nurse. This is what we did. Mary Ann enrolled as a day student, and I enrolled as a night student. We both hit the books real hard. Mary Ann was carrying 23 units per semester and I was carrying 16.

We both worked very hard to achieve good grades, especially Mary Ann. She would study night and day when she wasn't attending class. She did a lot of research at the library into the wee hours of the night. I would get out of bed at 4:30 a.m., and travel 50 miles to work. At night I would get home just in time to shower, grab a bite to eat, and then hit the road to attend classes. I maintained a 3.75 average, but after two semesters I had to drop out, I couldn't keep up with the pace. Mary Ann stuck it out, and graduated with a 4.0 average.

Mary Ann is a very smart person. During her college years, she worked part time as an aide at St. Jude Hospital in Fullerton. When she became an RN, she went to work at St Jude full time, and after only 6 weeks of working at St Jude, she was offered the Head Nurse's Job in the Cardiac ward. She debated for a long time before accepting the offer.

I became unemployed and restless. We had a beautiful home and beautiful furniture. But I was very lonely. Mary Ann tried to comfort me, but I was out of control. I was very abusive with Mary Ann, Edward, and Arnold. At the time, I thought that I was the only one going through this terrible ordeal. I did not realize that I was ignoring my two sons, whom I love very dearly. I was trying to escape reality, but didn't know how. Emotionally, I was exhausted from grief. Some of my fellow co-workers offered me some Benny Pills to help me concentrate. I began taking them and they did pep me up. I then began to drink much more than usual. The two combined really put me on a high. I committed acts that were totally absurd. I would drive by the parking lot at St. Jude Hospital and leave obscene notes on the windshield of Mary Ann's car. The consumption of alcohol and drugs was driving me out of my mind. I would leave home and stay gone for days. I would drive from Fullerton to Seattle on I-5, hoping to find whatever I was looking for. I guess it was just peace of mind.

When I became sleepy during my travels up and down I-5, I would pull off to the side of the road and try to rest my eyes. But I would be wide-awake from the pills that I was taking. I must have stopped at every truck stop between Fullerton and Seattle. I met lots of guys that seemed to be in similar situations. Back home in Fullerton, Mary Ann would be at work, and Edward and Arnold would be at school. I didn't want to go home to an empty house, so I would park in a nearby shopping mall across from St. Jude Hospital waiting for Mary Ann to get off from work. I would park where I could see her as she pulled out of the parking lot at St. Jude, and follow her home.

At home, she didn't greet me the way she used to greet me when I would be away from home. We would start arguing about the least little thing. I was a complete jerk. I don't know why we didn't get a divorce. If I hadn't been such a coward, I would probably have committed suicide. I felt like I had nothing to live for. I continued to visit with Chris. I kept expecting her to meet me any day.

I knew that I had to sober up, because of the state of our finances. Mary Ann was the only breadwinner, although I did have my VA benefits every month as a disabled veteran. We did okay, but I needed to get back to work to rebuild my character, my self worth. However, I wasn't ready to work for or take orders from another human being. I obtained a Contractors License and went into business for myself.

My first contract job was with Williams and Edwards Construction Company. Earl Williams and Stan Edwards were the owners. Earl and Stan were from Oklahoma. We had a lot in common and we became pretty good friends. Stan and his wife Bernice invited Mary Ann and me out to parties many times. Mary Ann wasn't a drinker, but I needed a partner to drink with, so she started drinking with me. It seemed that every week we went to the Golden West Ballroom for drinking and dancing.

We became addicted to the wild side of life and enjoyed every bit of it. I was still frustrated with life as I needed some answers and there wasn't anyone to turn to. Mary Ann was a responsible and dedicated person. But I was a total mess. I was too blind to learn from her that, living is the only answer.

Mary Ann and I saw to it that Edward and Arnold did not have to go without. We bought them new cars and saw to it that they had the very best clothes to wear. We even paid for their insurance and credit cards. We wanted them to have what we didn't have when we were their ages. I guess we were trying to make up for Chris and the things that she could have had.

I knew for a fact that I was on the verge of a nervous breakdown. One evening, while I was dreaming, Chris came walking up to me in a beautiful white dress. She was walking in a beautiful garden with golden lights. I remember most vividly the peacefulness of the scene bathed in Technicolor. She said to me, "Daddy I am okay." She then turned and walked back through this beautiful open gate circled with a halo of warm light. I awoke in a cold sweat, but the ghosts of my grief seemed to have diminished. I went back to sleep and slept for an awfully long time. The next morning, my mind seemed to be more at ease and my emotions in less turmoil. I knew that I had to get control and get on with my life.

That experience in my life is as vivid to me now as it was then. I feel there are many people "out there" who have had similar experiences, but who hesitate to tell anyone but their closest confidants, for fear of being thought of as over imaginative, slightly crazed, or worse! I believe now that my "visions" were not the product of an overactive mind but genuine spiritual experiences given to me for a purpose. I may learn just why someday.

Chapter 13

WHIDBEY ISLAND

In 1978, Mary Ann and I took a trip to Whidbey Island, Washington to visit with her mother, Helen, and sister, Margaret, and after returning to Fullerton, we decided to sell out and relocate on Whidbey Island. Mary Ann quit her job, and we put the house up for sale. Within a month the house sold. We had made a small fortune from the sale.

While waiting for the house to close, Mary Ann drove back to Whidbey to find us a house to rent. She did find one, and it was located on the west side of Whidbey Island with a spectacular view of Puget Sound looking up the Straits of Juan de Fuca to the Pacific Ocean. Mary Ann and I drove out to the mausoleum to say a goodbye for now to our little love. I threw her a kiss as we headed back to our house to see how the movers were doing. Mary Ann chuckled. The movers said that they would be loaded out by noon and would then be heading for Whidbey Island, Washington. Arnold our youngest son had already left for Whidbey. We had just bought him a new Chevrolet Blazer. Edward lived in San Jose working for a testing laboratory, and he was to join us on Whidbey at a later date.

As Mary Ann and I were leaving Fullerton, I felt very sad in leaving Chris. But I had come to realize that she would have agreed with our choice of moving. I also realized after all those years I had wept over the grave of our little love one taken from us by death., that her short stay with us was her shortest way to Heaven.

During our trip to Whidbey, Mary Ann and I discussed many issues, as to what our lives had been, and what the future held for us. We discussed the thought of building a house on Whidbey, among other things. We knew that this move would be the beginning of a new chapter in our lives. We had been though hell together and separately. I began to realize that for years I was unable to bridge the gap of loneliness, even though I still had Mary Ann, Edward, and Arnold. Unwittingly, I had dragged myself into a deeper ditch of despair and abandoned that family I loved so much while I nearly drowned in selfish desolation. I had acted without thought or sensitivity to those around me and, however unintentional, I had nearly destroyed our family. I hold *Deep Regrets* within.

We stopped in Everett, Washington the second night on the road and stayed at the Holiday Inn before going to Whidbey. The next morning we decided skip the ferry ride from Mukilteo, in south Everett, to Clinton on Whidbey Island. Instead we drove up through Mount Vernon, across to Fidalgo Island, through Deception Pass, onto Whidbey. This would be my first experience in a long time of driving on a two-lane road with slower drivers in front of me. However, we had decided to take life in a gentler manner if we could. We realized that we would have to get used to a slower pace on Whidbey compared to California's fast driving lanes.

When we arrived in Greenbank, at Loganberry Hill Realty, Helen, and Margaret greeted us. Our time of arrival was lunchtime, so we had lunch at the Loft above the Greenbank General Store. Mary Ann couldn't wait to show me this house that she had rented for us. It was located on the west side of Whidbey just off Smugglers' Cove Road. She asked that I park the car off on the side of the road, and that we walk down the entrance road to the house. When we got within sight of the house, she asked that I close my eyes, and hold her hand, and she would tell me when to open my eyes. We walked the remaining distance down an incline. I was getting a bit uncomfortable.

"OK you can open your eyes now."

This house was so unique. It was situated on five acres of

land with a spectacular view of the Puget Sound. I was really impressed with her choice. It was secluded and romantic. The owner of the house lived in Canada, and his last name was Moore. We always referred to the house as the Moore's house.

Three days later we received a call from Bekins Movers. They had arrived on Whidbey, and wanted me to direct them in getting to the Moore's House. They were in Clinton, and had just gotten off the ferry. They didn't have any problems finding the house. They seem to be pretty exhausted, and it was pouring down rain, so they asked if they take a nap in the truck before they started unloading. It was no problem. Mary Ann instructed them where to put things when they did start off loading.

We went back to Loganberry Hill Realty, and spent the rest of the day with Helen and Margaret. That evening Margaret invited us to have dinner at Paul's Landing. At Paul's our waitress, Kathy Bennett, greeted us with the utmost courtesy. The food and service was great. So we choose Paul's place to eat every Friday evening, and we always requested that Kathy be our waitress.

I really had a time with the owner of Paul's because he thought that I was the same Charles Herring, who was a commentator on King 5, television station. By having the same name, it really served its purpose when I would make reservations for a Hotel room in Seattle. It was fun!

We spent the night at Margaret's, and went back to the Moore house early the next morning. When we arrived, the moving men had just about everything off loaded and put in the right rooms, more or less. They said, "We should be done with the unloading by noon." They finally finished, and began trying to get up the hill on the muddy driveway. They were unable to do so because of the heavy downfall of rain. The road was miserable. We had to call a guy in to have their truck pulled out with a tractor.

Over the next week, we got everything unpacked and put it in its proper place, and began to enjoy the aesthetics of Whidbey Island. Margaret introduced us to several of her friends; one in particular was Helen Sparr. We attended lots of parties at Helen Sparr's house. She was a great entertainer.

Our friends Stan and Bernice Edwards from California often came to Whidbey to visit with us. Richard and Virginia had moved from California to Brinnon, Washington. Our close relationship preceded us. We lived at the Moore's house for one year and in the meantime Mary Ann and I started back to work. She went to work at Everett General Hospital in Everett, and I went to work for Cannon Construction at the Boeing facility at Paine Field. Our son Arnold went to work for the Nichols Brothers, commercial boat builders, in Freeland.

Construction on the American Legion Hall in Bayview, also known as Whidbey City, had just begun. We were in need of a place for entertainment. We, among others, were delighted when it was opened. When our friends, Stan and Bernice, from California came to visit with us, we would always take them to the Legion.

Stan said, "It's quite an asset to the south end of Whidbey."

Our favorite place for dining was still Paul's Landing. We would always take Stan and Bernice there. Paul and Bob Stilnovich, the owners, always greeted our friends with warmth. Kathy Bennett, our favorite waitress, always was most hospitable to our friends and us.

Stan remarked, "Kathy always makes us feel really comfortable," which meant a lot to them, and to Mary Ann and me as well.

Things were going well for Mary Ann and me again, but after living at the Moore's house for a year, we decided that we should start looking around for a house to buy, because we only had eighteen months to buy or build if we wanted to avoid paying a Capital Gains Tax. So we bought two lots from friends of ours, at Lagoon Point. This purchase was an exceptional buy for us. Our friends had tried for years to get the lots to perk, but weren't able to do so. They would always have the person with a backhoe dig the perk test hole in the hardpan soil near the road. From the lot, there was a 180-degree view of Puget

Sound and the Olympic Mountains across Admiralty Inlet. All of the major ships passed by going into the ports Seattle, Everett, Bremerton, and Tacoma and, of course, the submarines to Bangor naval base.

We made an offer for the two lots, and they accepted our offer. However, being they were friends of ours, they warned us about the lots not perking. I assured them that that would not be a problem. I called Hanford Thayer, who was a civil engineer here on Whidbey, and he too thought that I was the Charles Herring from King 5 television. He assured me that he could get the lots to perk. We closed the deal with Lorna and Mel. Hanford came out with a post hole digger and dug a hole 3 feet deep at the base of the lots. He got a beautiful 3-bedroom perk from it. Hanford submitted the results to Island County, and then we applied for a permit to build our dream house.

Before buying the lots at Lagoon Point, we had made an offer to buy the Moore's house, but he didn't want to sell at the time. We decided not to renew our lease with the Moore's, so we had to find another place to live while waiting on our permit to build at Lagoon Point and the actual construction of the house. So Mary Ann found a nice house to rent on Donahey Road in Greenbank. And we lived there for the next year.

Construction work in Washington was booming. Boeing was really expanding their facilities. So I decided to obtain my Contractors License and to go into the steel business placing reinforcing steel and erecting structural steel. Our first job was with Sellen Construction Company, on the John Fluke Building in Everett. It was the consensus of everyone that we name our company, Island Steel Erectors, Inc. Arnold quit his job at Nichols Brothers, and Edward quit his job in San Jose, California, and came up to join us.

Mary Ann got busy trying to find a house plan that we would like. When she did find the one that we liked, I congratulated her with her selection. It was a nice 5 bedroom two story house with approximately 3700 square feet. The concept of the house was fine, but Mary Ann wanted to make some changes by adding to and deleting from some of the areas.

The original concept of the living room was to be an eight-foot flat ceiling. But she converted it into a cathedral ceiling with an exposed wood beam at the peak of the ceiling. She designed a six-foot wide fireplace extending from the bottom of the footing to the top of the house. There was a fireplace down stairs and one upstairs. She changed the original concept of the windows. There were only a few indicated on the original plans. She added windows throughout the entire house, especially in the living room, dining room, and kitchen areas, so that we could enjoy the spectacular view of the entire sound.

After Mary Ann had completed reorganizing the plans to our satisfaction, we began looking for a contractor to build our dream home. Little did we know that we were fixing to enter into the Twilight Zone. Bids were put out to three prospective house builders. They all responded, but they would not be able to start construction for about 6 months. Hanford Thayer knew of our urgency, so he recommended a builder. He said, "I didn't know this builder personally, but only that he at least is available to start building immediately."

We called the person that Hanford had recommended to determine whether he would be interested in bidding on the construction of our house. He said that he was, so we set up an appointment with him to review our house plans. We met with him and gave him a set of plans to review, emphasizing our schedule.

Three days later we received a call from the builder stating that he was completed with his estimate, and that he would like to meet with Mary Ann and me to submit his bid. His proposal was substantially lower than any of the other bidders. He said that the construction of the house from start to finish would be completed in three months. We were satisfied with his proposal and accepted him as the person to build our dream home.

Construction of our dream home started on time. Our builder had selected all of the subcontractors that were to perform. Excavation began, and shortly afterwards the footings were poured. The framing began to go up. Mary Ann and I were very happy with the progress that was being made.

In the evenings after work, Mary Ann and I would stop by the house to see how much progress had been accomplished for that day. One evening we noticed something that didn't look quite right. Some of the framing of the walls in the kitchen area was not plumb, even to the naked eye. I check the tolerance with my level, and in some cases the walls were out of plumb as much as a 1/4 inch to the foot. A wall of 8 feet high would mean that the wall would be out of plumb by 2 inches, which was not acceptable to the building code or to my satisfaction.

I placed a call to our builder to inform him of the out of plumb situation, and he assured me that he would take care of it. However, he never did take care of it. His lack of workmanship was beginning to show up in other parts of the house. There were days when he or his workers didn't even show up for work. His excuse was that he had underbid the construction of our house, and he had to work on another house to help pay his crew. He abandoned our house, so I hired a lawyer and terminated our builder's contract.

Our attorney was a lawyer in Freeland. Our builder obtained a lawyer by the name of Jackson, in Edmonds, Washington, and sued me for breach of contract. Our lawyer said that this lawsuit of our builder was absurd. How can a person be sued for breach of contract, when it was the plaintiff who breached our contract by abandonment? He said that we would win this lawsuit hands down.

In the meantime, our house needed to be completed. Our lawyer recommended Gary Bostrom, who was a house builder at the time. Gary submitted a price to finish our house in the amount of $20,000.00, more than what our original builder had estimated. The additional $20,000.00 was over our budget, so we had to go to Washington Federal in Oak Harbor, Washington to apply for a loan. Washington Federal was a little reluctant at first. They wanted some assurance that we would win the lawsuit. So our lawyer wrote them a letter on our behalf assuring them that we would win this lawsuit.

Gary came in and started making the necessary corrections on the error that our first builder had made. He then began to finish the construction of our house. Gary had two employee's working with him. They finished our house on time, and with great workmanship. Mary Ann and I were very happy with their performance. However, so that Gary could finish certain portions of the house, he had to call some of the subcontractors' back in to finish their work, and they wouldn't come back unless I paid them money that was due them from our builder. I didn't appreciate having to repay all the subcontractors again, but I did.

Mary Ann and I didn't need or deserve what was about to come. Our lawyer called and said that he had received a summons for us to appear in arbitration on a certain date. He suggested that we meet with him and Gary Bostrom at his office to prepare for arbitration. Mary Ann and I felt comfortable with the strategy that our lawyer and Gary had assured us we would win without any problems.

Our lawyer called Mary Ann and me to inform us that a calendar date of March 1, 1981, had been set for us to attend arbitration in down town Seattle. The morning of arbitration Mary Ann, and I met with our lawyer, Gary Bostrom, and one of Gary's employee's in the waiting room of the arbitration building. The arbitrator was not a lawyer he was a retired Architect, whose name I have forgotten. His secretary greeted us with a cup of coffee, and invited us into the conference room. Our builder and his wife were already waiting in the conference room accompanied by their attorney. They both had a very pitiful look on their faces, and they were wearing emblems of the cross, and a picture of Jesus Christ.

The arbitrator entered the room, and introduced himself, and said that the meeting was now open for discussion, and the attorney for the plaintiff could proceed with his argument for his clients. The silly questions that were asked by our builder's attorney, such as why Mr. Herring, did you expect your builder to have your house completed in three months? My response was because our builder agreed to a three-month schedule as per contract. Mr. Herring why didn't you pay your builder his progress payments? My response was that I did pay our builder his progress payment up until he abandoned the job.

This line of questioning went on back and forth all day long. At the end of the closing day, we adjourned until the next day at 9:00 a.m. The next day was basically the same as the first day. I didn't feel as if we had accomplished anything the day before and it appeared to me that we weren't going to accomplish anything on this second day. I was right. We adjourned, and the arbitrator said to the attorney's that they would be notified of our next meeting.

Three weeks later we received a call from our lawyer stating that a calendar date had been set for our next hearing. The location was to be in the Northwest Construction Council building near Fisherman's Terminal in Seattle. This was fine with us, because I was a member of the Northwest Construction Council. Parking would be no problem because of my membership.

On the day of the hearing, Mary Ann and I met with our lawyer, Gary, and his employee in the parking lot of the Northwest Construction Council. We entered the building with great confidence. Our lawyer said that the arbitrator would probably render his decision on this day.

As we entered the conference room, I thought we'd entered a church. The only thing missing was the collection plate, but that would come later. Our builder and his wife were sitting at this oval conference table accompanied by their attorney and a co-worker that had worked on our house with our builder. He and his wife were both decorated with emblems of the cross, and she was holding a bible in her hands.

The hearing got underway, and everyone was sworn in. The arbitrator asked to hear from the witnesses first. Our first builder's co-worker started off by saying that in two years our house would be valued at $250,000. I could see a sigh of relief in the arbitrator's eyes. At the time I didn't understand the relevance of his testimony, and why was his testimony so germane to this hearing. I soon found out.

The hearing lasted for about two hours. The arbitrator said

that he would consider all of the evidence, and would render his decision within two weeks. After the hearing adjourned, I invited our lawyer, Gary, and his employee to lunch in the cafeteria down stairs of the building. While we were having lunch, our lawyer spoke up and said that at one time this is where he had lunch with Jean Enerson. Jean is the newscaster on King 5 Television. He said that he had gone to school with her at Stanford. He told us that she'd said, that to get anywhere in life, one had to have a gimmick.

On or about two weeks later, we received a call from our lawyer, saying that the verdict had come in from the arbitrator, and that it was not good. The verdict favored our original builder, and I was to pay him another $8,000, because this was the amount owing to him when he abandoned the job. Boy! What a shocker. Our lawyer said that the arbitrator's decision was not right or fair, and somewhere down the line this would tell on him. I didn't understand what he meant by this statement, and still don't as of this day.

At the time, I didn't have $8,000 to pay our "builder". So I did the next best thing, I called my friend Stan Edwards in California, and explained my situation to him, and I asked him for a loan. He said no problem that he would send it right away. He didn't even ask the question as to when I would repay him. I did tell him that I would repay him when we received our next monthly draw from the business. I did repay him with some interest.

Mary Ann and I were still baffled over the arbitrator's verdict. We couldn't understand where we had gone wrong. So, out of curiosity, I called our "builder's" lawyer. I wanted some answers to my questions, so I began by congratulating him in his winning of the case. To my surprise, he said, that we had the winning case, but our lawyer just wasn't experienced enough to handle a case like this one.

I informed our lawyer of my conversation with our builder's lawyer. He said that he didn't know what he was talking about. I asked our lawyer to appeal on our behalf, and he said that he would think about it. One evening about 10:00 p.m. I received a call from our lawyer saying that he would like to be paid for his services that he had rendered on our behalf. I reminded him of the $2,000.00 that I had paid him up front. And our agreement was that in the event we won the case, he was to receive 25% from our award. So since we received zero percent, he would receive zero percent. He became very upset, and hung up the phone on me.

A few days later, I received a call from our lawyer. He asked that I meet with him at the Blueberry Hills Restaurant for lunch. He said that he had a lawyer friend that he wanted me to meet. I agreed to have lunch with them. I arrived and waited for their arrival. When they did arrive, our lawyer said, "Chuck I would like you to meet Larry Shafer. Larry is a trial lawyer, and he is a self-made lawyer, he lives here on Whidbey."

During our lunch, our lawyer said that he wanted to withdraw from representing me in this case, and that he recommended Larry very highly to serve as his replacement for him. He asked if it would be okay with me for Larry to replace him. I said that this would be fine with me. Larry began telling me of his background, and suggested that Mary Ann and I meet with him and his wife Jackie, who was a lawyer also, at Paul's landing at Bush Point for dinner that evening. I agreed.

When Mary Ann and I arrived at Paul's Landing, Larry was already seated, having a beer. I introduced Larry to Mary Ann. He said that Jackie would be arriving any time soon. She had been in Court all day in Coupeville. Mary Ann and I ordered our usual drink while waiting for Jackie. When she arrived, she apologized for being late. Our first impression of Jackie was of the highest esteem. She was a delightful lady. We ordered our dinners, and spent a very enjoyable evening at Paul's.

Larry filed an appeal with the Court on our behalf. But because of the statute of limitation, it was not filed on time with the Court. However, Larry persuaded the Judge in Coupeville to hear our case. When our builder received notice of the hearing, he had a mild heart attack, so said his lawyer. The hearing was all in vain. The Judge was not about to overrule the arbitrator's decision, and that was that.

A few years later, our real builder, Gary Bostrom ran for Island County Commissioner of South Whidbey and won. Gary committed suicide at a later date. [Reasons unknown to me].

In 1980, funds were appropriated by the State of Washington to construct a new high school on south Whidbey. The school board advertised for bids from various general contractors. Farmer Construction Company from Canada was the apparent low bidder, so they were awarded the contract. And we, Island Steel Erectors, Inc. were the low bidders for placing the reinforcing steel, and erecting the structural steel. This was a very nice job for us.

Bill Orr was the general superintendent for Farmers Construction. Bill developed melanoma cancer before the job was over and died. We completed our work but with a grain of sadness.

In the summer of 1979, Edward, my son had met a young student nurse by the name of Mary Jo. She was introduced to him through Chris, the wife of Edward's cousin Tommy. Chris and Mary Jo were attending nursing school together at Everett Community College in Everett, Washington. Mary Jo is from Decatur, Indiana.

On November 29, 1980, our beloved pet Nikie had to be put to sleep. Edward, Mary Jo, Arnold, and I took him to the Vet in Clinton where she injected him with a shot to put him to sleep. Before we left Edward's house, I asked of Edward and Arnold to try to control their emotions. As I watched the vet putting Nikie to sleep, I had a flash back of Christina asking to see Nikie before she died. I broke down and began to cry like a baby. After Nikie had been put to sleep, I placed his little lifeless body in a large plastic bag, and took him back to our house and built a coffin, and buried him in the front yard of our house. Nikie had lived with us for 18 years; he was a part of our family.

Edward and Mary Jo united their lives in Holy Matrimony on June 12, 1982. They were married in Clinton, Washington, on Whidbey Island. This was a very happy day for the Herrings and for Mary's family. Mary's family drove out from Decatur, Indiana to attend the wedding. Our families hit it off very well from the start. We really enjoyed Mary Jo's grandfather. He was a gentleman and a scholar. He obviously had great affection for Mary. It was a sad day when they all had to pack up and go back to Decatur. They really made us feel as if they had accepted us as part of their family.

In June of 1987, Edward and Mary took a vacation, and traveled throughout the southern states where all of my folks were living and they all welcomed Mary into our family. I think Mary felt comfortable meeting them. From there they went to visit Mary's family in Decatur. On June 17, which was Father's day that year, I received a call from Edward, presenting me a gift that any father would want to receive. I would soon be promoted (about time I got one) to grandfather. Mary was pregnant with a little girl. I was so overwhelmed with this joyful news I could hardly speak. I thanked God for sending this little girl to our family.

On February 11, 1988, Edward and Mary were blessed with the birth of their precious daughter, Annie. We all cherish the ground that Annie walks on. I felt as if God had sent Annie to all of us to help fill the void in Mary Ann's and my life. From the moment she was born, she could do no wrong in my eyes. I love her with all of my heart. Annie is now 14 years old, and in the 8th grade.

On July 10, 1996, Edward and Mary were blessed with another precious child. His name is Shawn. His grandparents dote on him.

Over the next few years, the workload for Island Steel Erectors increased rapidly. Edward had decided that he would like to become a photographer, so he retired from the ironworking trade, and started back to school, to become a professional photographer. He served an apprenticeship with a well-known photographer by the name of Michael Jay, from Oak Harbor, Washington. I am so proud of Edward's achievement in his business. Every year he displays his talents at the Island County Fair in Langley, Washington. I love him very dearly.

Mary Ann's brother, Bill died on the same date that our

daughter Christina died, which was April 8. Chris died in 1970 and Bill in 1982. Mary Ann's mother Helen passed away on Ed, and Bernice's' anniversary, June 24, 1989. Mary Ann's sister Bernice passed away on Helen's, birthday, April 9, 1990.

My brother Gene died on June 22, 1990. He was 56 years old, and died of lung cancer. My dad died on November 13, 1990. My mother died on July 19, 1995. All of the deceased members of Mary Ann's and my family have been tremendously missed. Our prayers are with them all.

I put these numbers together and have wondered if they are of any significance. I know that we buried our beloved daughter Chris on the 11th day of the month. And our first two grandkids were born on the 11th day of the month. And our youngest grandson was born one day short of the 11th. He was born on the 10th day of the month. Maybe I should consult a numerologist. The ancient Romans sure believed in numerology and they were pretty smart.

I have always encouraged my sons, Edward and Arnold, to choose their profession, what ever they might be. I told them not to let my influence sway them one way or another. I was happy that Edward chose to become a Photographer. Arnold and I both missed him very much when he left Island Steel. But, as it turned out, he made the right choice for himself, and I am very proud of him.

On September 5, 1990, Arnold, and his girlfriend, Lois, were joined together in the bonds of Holy Matrimony at Fern Grotto, in Kauai. Before their marriage, Arnold took off work from Island Steel, so that he and Lois could build their dream home. After they completed building their dream home, they left for Hawaii to tie the knot. Arnold's friend, Jim, had assisted Arnold with the framing of their house. This would be the first house that Arnold had ever built. He always said that he knew that he could do it. He had said that if he had it to do over, instead of being an ironworker, he would probably have chosen to be a carpenter.

On March 11, 1992, Lois gave birth to their first-born son, and our second grandchild, Jeffery. As we did with Annie, we fell in love with Jeffery. He was such a delightful little boy. Jeffery is now 10 years old, and is in the 4th grade. We love him dearly.

Annie, and her cousin, Jeffery, were very good for one another. They shared nearly everything they did. They were more like brother and sister then cousins. Mary Ann and I really became attached to them. They were at grandma's house every day, except when their parents weren't working. Annie and Jeffery really filled a void in our life as they were growing up.

All the holidays for several years were spent at our house. Mary Ann has always enjoyed cooking dinners for everyone. She is a great cook among her other attributes (my girth is living proof of that) such as being a loving and caring grandma and the best wife any man could ever hope for.

Chapter 14

Island Steel Erectors work load increased tremendously over the next several years. But it got to be where we had to have a lawyer on our payroll at all times. The steel fabricators that were supplying the steel for our jobs were pretty much overloaded in most cases, so they would ship the steel to the job site without checking to see if they had made any mistakes. And of course, when they did make a mistake, they would expect us to correct it for them at no charge. Some of the mistakes we did correct at no charge, but there were some fabricators that couldn't get any thing right from start to finish. We just had to charge them to correct their mistakes, and of course that made us the bad guys. They would always say, well you guys should have bid high enough to take care of any mistakes that we make. I would always remind them of my competitors, and what the consequences would be if we were to bid high. It was very simply; we wouldn't get the job and they wouldn't get our orders.

Some of the general contractors would never honor a subcontract; even when they agreed to do so at bid time. They were worse than the steel fabricators. When engineers gave us the wrong elevations or wrong lines, which were always a problem for Island Steel as well as with all of my competitors, we would never accept the responsibility for the engineering of their jobs. However, they expected us to stand around with a crew of ironworkers, and a crane on standby at anywhere between $75 and $125/hour, depending on the size of the crane we were renting, just waiting for them to correct their mistakes at no charge. At the time we were paying an Ironworker including benefits at a rate of $39 per hour. These losses add up very quickly.

The worst of all was Bow Construction Company. They would authorize extra work, and sign for it, but when it became time for them to pay for their extra work, they would renege, and offer $.35 on the dollar; knowing that it would cost a subcontractor that and much more just for a lawyer. Other general contractors adopted this crooked strategy.

Island Steel's last few years weren't all that pleasant. Its last big job was the federal detention center at Sea-Tac, Washington. USA Construction Company was the prime contractor for the United States Bureau of Prisons. On this job, Island Steel Erectors was operating under Phoenix Steel Erectors. Phoenix originally intended to subcontract directly with USA for provision and erection of structural steel and precast concrete on the project. Ratty Steel out of Dallas, Texas intended to fabricate and supply the steel to Phoenix for incorporation into the Project. But because Phoenix was unable to provide a bond as required by USA, Ratty and Phoenix switched places, with Ratty contracting directly with USA, and Phoenix becoming a second tier subcontractor to Ratty.

The oncoming version of this story is dedicated to all subcontractors, and especially to Steel Erectors throughout. I had previously spoken with my brother-in-law's brother, Oral Limehouse, who is the owner of On Line Metal Products, Inc. in Southern California. Oral had said that he and Ratty Steel had been working together for the past eight years, and that he was satisfied with Ratty's performance.

I believed Oral, so being in need of a good steel fabricator, I placed a call to the owner of Ratty Steel in Dallas, Texas. I asked him if he would be interested in working with me here in the Northwest. He said that he would be happy to work with me and, as a matter of fact, that he had just hired a project manager by the name of Jack Simpson to work in this area. He would have Jack call me.

On or about August 5, 1994, I received a call from Jack, informing me that he had been told to contact me, so that we could bid on the Federal Detention Center at Sea-Tac, Washington together.

I bought the plans and specifications for this project, and welcomed Jack into our office located at Mukilteo, Washington. We provided Jack with office space to work, with a desk, fax, telephone, and a copier. We immediately begin working on the Federal Detention Center project. It took us about three weeks to complete our estimates. The bid date was on September 14, 1994 at 2:00 PM.

On December 5, 1994, USA and Ratty Steel entered into a contract with Phoenix Steel as a second tier subcontractor to Ratty Steel. After the signing of the Ratty/Phoenix contract dated February 8, 1995, things began to deteriorate. Jack Simpson was no longer project manager for Ratty. The owner had appointed a Toyota used-car salesman to replace Jack. This guy, with no experience whatsoever was put out into the field of trying to manage a pre-cast and structural steel job here in the Northwest. It was beyond comprehension. Yet, this guy was sent out to educate all of us structural steel and pre-cast people on how great he was because he knew nothing else, it seemed.

This new project manager had asked that Phoenix Steel mobilize on the job in mid February 1995, which was five months early. His reason for early mobilization was that since it was their first job here in the Northwest, they wanted to impress USA Construction of their high capabilities. Their intentions were to fabricate, and ship to the job site all of the structural steel, so that when USA was ready for erection, we would be on the job site, and ready to meet their schedule. He had assured Phoenix that for any standby time incurred, Ratty would pay Phoenix up and beyond its contract price.

On March 2, 1995, I sent four ironworkers to the job site ready to start work on the mock-up walls. They were unable to start on the mock-up walls because USA was nowhere ready for them. USA was totally unprepared, they had not stripped the forms for the walls, nor had any of the embeds been cleaned. We couldn't erect any pre-cast panels. We had to send two of the men home, and had to pay them two hours show-up time.

As things turned out, it was a total disaster between Ratty and Phoenix. Ratty in my opinion turned out to be the worst steel fabricator that I had ever dealt with, bar none. They couldn't get anything detailed right nor could they deliver on time as promised. USA insisted on a second shift, and consequently Phoenix was put square in the middle, since Phoenix had bid the job based on a standard 5 day, 40 hour week, Monday through Friday, from 7:00 a.m. to 4:30 p.m. with no money in the budget for a second shift whatsoever.

This dilemma turned into a snowball that would not stop rolling downhill. Things were increasingly out of control. Ratty had to sub out the major proportion of the fabrication to another local steel fabricator because they couldn't keep up with the two-shift schedule. Phoenix was spending more out of pocket money for the extras, than it was on its regular payroll. Phoenix could not continue without compensation. It was not getting paid, so Phoenix had to pull off of the job for non-payment and breach of contract. From July 26, 1995, through October 10, 1995, Phoenix had expended out of pocket money on extras alone in the amount of $40,128.00. It was October 10, 1995, when Phoenix had to leave the job.

Ratty took over the erection, and I agreed to leave our equipment and crews on the job until Ratty could buy their own. However, we never recovered all of our equipment. Ratty kept most of it.

The oncoming version of this story is the worst mistake I have ever made in my entire life. I filed a lawsuit against Ratty Steel. Arnold and I debated about what we should do regarding this mess with Ratty Steel. I suggested that we file a lawsuit against Ratty, since we had the evidence on our side, and thus try to recoup our losses.

Mr. John Bonds, an attorney with one of the larger law firms in Seattle, was recommended as someone we should select to represent us in this lawsuit. I placed a call to John, and briefly discussed our case over the phone. We set a time for an appointment, which was the following Monday morning at 10:

00 a.m. John asked that I fax to him the nature of our case, so that he would have time to review it over the week-end.

When Arnold and I arrived at John's office in downtown Seattle, his secretary greeted us, and she asked if we would like to have a cup of coffee. She asked us to have a seat and that John was expecting us and that he would be right with us. We sat for a while until John came out and greeted us. He invited us into his conference room. We sat at chairs in the conference room and the first thing that John said was that, "He was glad that he wasn't representing Ratty Steel in this case." In other words we had the winning case.

Arnold and I felt very comfortable with John, and for once in our lives, we had a winning case. We spent about an hour with John going over the details. After hearing Arnold and me out, he agreed to represent Phoenix Steel, and that he would keep in touch.

During the month of August 1995, several letters were written back and forth to Ratty. For the month August, John invoiced us in the amount of $1,207.50. I cut a check and mailed it to him immediately.

Little did I know at the time of what John's intentions were? I never heard from him for several months afterwards. I called his office daily trying to speak with him. We wanted to know what was taking place with our lawsuit. However, John never did return my phone calls. In the meantime, I received a call from the owner of Ratty Steel, he said, "Chuck, I have just gotten off of the phone with John Bonds. I called him to represent me in this lawsuit, and he said that he could not represent me because of his commitment to you. But he recommended that I contact another law firm there in Seattle. But, he also said that since his law firm was representing USA, that he would not be able to represent you either."

You can imagine how I felt after talking with Ratty Steel. I was really frustrated. Here we were ready to go for broke. But then to hear this kind of news coming from our enemy, and not from the lawyer, in whom we had put all our trust, was indeed, quite discouraging and angering. I immediately tried calling

John, but his secretary said that he wasn't in, so I left a message on his voice mail for him to return my call.

At the time I did not know about Rule 1.3—Diligence—whereby a lawyer shall act with reasonable diligence and promptness in representing a client. Also, I was not aware of the Rule 4.62, whereby suspension is generally appropriate when a lawyer knowingly deceives a client and/or cause's injury or potential injury to the client.

After several months of trying to call, and leaving messages on John's voice mail, he finally did call back near the end of February, 1996. To my disappointment, he reiterated what the owner of Ratty Steel had said. He said was that he wouldn't be able to represent us in this case because of our insolvent position. Also, since their law firm represented USA, there would be a conflict of interest.

However, John said that he had contacted a lawyer by the name of Earl Tiptop, and that he has explained our "winning case" to Mr. Tiptop. He explained that Mr. Tiptop would be willing to represent us on a "contingency" basis, meaning that the lawyer representing a client does so without a fee but, he will receive a certain percentage of the award granted by the courts.

We had no choice in the matter, so I placed a call to Earl Tiptop, and left a message on his voice mail. Later on in the day he returned my call, and said that he would be happy to represent us, because he was mainly concerned with justice, and that John had said that we had the winning case. So we set up an appointment to meet with Earl on March 1, 1996.

The name of Earl's law firm was Tiptop Attorneys at Law in Seattle on First Street. As Arnold and I entered Earl's reception area, we were greeted much the same as we were when we entered John's office. His secretary offered us a cup of coffee, and said that Mr. Tiptop would be right with us. We didn't have to wait long. Earl greeted us with a nice smile and a manly handshake. He asked that we step into his office.

The view from his office was breath taking. Arnold and I were really impressed with the arrangement of his office. He seemed to be very well organized. We began exchanging our backgrounds. He seemed to be very knowledgeable, and a well-educated lawyer. We were impressed with his neat appearance, and his being a family man.

It was on this date March 1, 1996, that we engaged Earl to represent us with our claim against Ratty Steel on the Federal Corrections Facility Project in Sea-Tac, Washington. We were suing for breach of contract and wrongful construction termination. I vividly remember saying to Earl, if you don't think we have the winning case, let's not pursue, because of my insolvent situation. At which time, Earl said, "No doubt, you have the winning case."

After leaving Earl's office, Arnold and I were thrilled over Earl agreeing to represent us. We were really impressed with his eagerness to start working. And he did. He immediately filed a lawsuit against Ratty Steel. Ratty's law firm responded. Their lawyer that would be handling the case was a young man by the name of Greg Harley.

I will never forget the phone call that I received from Earl He was so excited to learn that this lawyer was representing Ratty by the name of Greg Harley. His words from day one was that he and Ralph, his partner, were really happy that Greg was Ratty's lawyer, because in their opinion, Greg was a stupid lawyer, and that he and Ralph would (verbatim) "clean his plow."

The lawyers began exchanging letters. Earl really flooded the mail with one letter after another. Arnold and I were really impressed with Earl's eagerness. And it did appear at the time that the defendants' left hand didn't know what the right hand was doing.

Earl wrote a letter to Greg Harley on May 24, 1996 stating, "That the enclosed is a stipulation and order referring the matter to arbitration and staying it pending issuance of the award. I understand from your phone call that the court advised that a joint status report would not be necessary. I signed the stipulation and order. If it is acceptable with you, please sign it and file it with court. If it is unacceptable to you, please call me so we may discuss your comments."

"I note that Burl Freeman has appeared as counsel for Love Insurance. I believe that only one of your signatures is necessary, because you have both appeared on behalf of Love. However, by copy of this letter, I am providing Mr. Freeman with a copy of the stipulation and order. I look forward to receiving a copy of the completely executed stipulation."

Additionally, in our phone call today, I advised you that Phoenix' response to the demand for arbitration appeared to be due on Sunday, Mary 26, 1996, and that I would therefore file the response on Tuesday, May 28. You said that this was acceptable to you.

Yours faithfully, Earl Tiptop"

Before proceeding with arbitration, Arnold and I had to submit $4,350 out of pocket, money payable to the AAA (meaning American Arbitration Association), and, in the event our case didn't go to arbitration, we were assured that our $4,350 would be refunded. As it turned out, we didn't go to arbitration, and our $4,350 was never returned. Earl Tiptop kept our money, and spent it on his "so called" expenses.

On July 23, 1996, I received a letter from Earl, informing me of mediation being scheduled on August 26, 1996, at 9:30 a.m. at the American Arbitration offices in Seattle. I should be advised that I would have to budget $750 for the mediation. The mediator, Mr. Brown's, fee would be $175 per hour.

One evening at home, I received a phone call from the owner of Ratty Steel. He said that he didn't want to go to court, and offered me $30,000.00 to cancel my lawsuit. This call was on a Thursday. He asked that I think about his offer, and call him by Monday morning. I hesitated about calling him, so he called me on Monday, kicking his offer up to $50,000.00. I flat out refused his offer.

I immediately called Earl to inform him of the offer that Ratty had made. I told him that I flatly refused his offer. Earl said, that's good, I'm glad you refused his offer, because I feel certain the minimum amount the court will allow us is $300,000.00.

So we proceeded with mediation. And the very first words out of the mediator's mouth were that he would like us to settle this case at his discretion, because he had never lost a case in his entire career and he didn't want to start now. It was like a three-ring circus. This mediator bounced back and forth between Ratty and ourselves; trying to get us to compromise with his suggestions. Well, as it turned out, he wasn't able to bring us together with a meeting of minds. He was very disappointed.

Preparation for trail began. Dick Silly was the residing Judge at the United States District Court for the Western District of Washington at Seattle, Washington. In preparing for this case there were so many documents compiled. On November 6, 1997, we were notified to appear in court. This would be our day in court.

As we gathered in the courtroom waiting for the Judge to enter, sipping a drink of water that had been placed for us to drink. I asked the question, as to why we were not served with coffee as well as water. Earl said that the Federal Courts didn't allow coffee. Don't ask me why.

The doors opened from the Judge's chambers, and the clerk asked that we all rise. The Judge entered like Zorro with his big black robe on. He then asked that we be seated. His first comment was that you lawyers have only three days to present this case, because I have a plane to catch, and be with my children on Thanksgiving Day. Arnold and I couldn't believe what we were hearing. After all of our time, and efforts, and spending thousands of dollars, we were only granted three days. WOW!

I was called to the stand, and Earl began asking me certain questions, and the Judge immediately cut his legs right out from under him. He wanted Earl to get to the facts. From that point on it was down hill for Earl. I kind of felt sorry for him, because the judge had really intimidated him to a point of no return.

Earl was alone; he didn't have his partner Ralph with him. Earl was relying heavily on Ralph for support. I think Ralph was the smarter member of their law firm. Ralph had ventured off elsewhere. Where, I don't know. Greg Harley, the lawyer for Ratty really worked Earl over. The shoe was on the other foot. From day one, Earl had said, "That he and Ralph would really stomp Greg, in a court of law."

One could tell from the Judge's demeanor that he favored the bigger law firm. After three days of testimony from all concerns. The Judge said that, "This case is so complicated, and you lawyers have really messed things up something terrible, I am not going to rule in favor of either of your clients. Therefore, my judgment is with prejudice. This means that, applied to orders of judgment dismissing a case, the plaintiff is forever barred from bringing a lawsuit on the same claim or cause.

Judge Silly's decision was a total shock to all concerned. I said to the owner of Ratty, that I should have accepted your last offer of $50,000. He said, "Yes you should have." We should have won this case on a "quantum meruit" ruling; an action brought for the value of the services rendered the defendant when there was no express contract as to the payment to be made. Judge Silly had already stated that there was never a contract between Ratty and Phoenix because there was never a meeting of the minds.

We all left the court crying in our beer. All the money we had spent trying to defend ourselves was down the tubes. The only ones that benefited from it all were the lawyers.

On November 10, 1997, I received a letter from Earl, expressing his disappointment with the Judge's decision. He encouraged me to appeal, because in his opinion, the Judge erred. He offered to represent me with an appeal providing that I pay him an additional $20,000.00 up front. I told him to get lost. I felt like vomiting while I was talking with him. I reminded him that if the Judge erred, then he should appeal on our behalf anyway. Even up until the 11th hour, Earl had boasted about how he and Ralph would take Greg Harley to the cleaners.

I did try to appeal on my own behalf as a "pro se" litigant, but a corporation ordinarily must be represented by an attorney and cannot carry on litigation "pro se."

I submitted motion after motion to Judge Silly, pleading for him to hear me out in my version as to what really happened regarding the situation between Ratty and Phoenix, because there was no one in the court that understood construction as well as Arnold or myself. But time after time he denied my request. It got to the point that he issued a court order for me to stop submitting any motions to the court whatsoever.

Even with the real evidence that I have, he still denied my motions. Such as "CONFISCATED PROPORTIONS OF PLANTIFF'S PERSONAL EQUIPMENT, LARCENY, PERJURY, FRAUD, FALSE CERTIFICATION, USE OF MAILS TO PROMOTE FRAUD, SWINDLES AND CONFIDENCE GAMES, INTENT, NEGLIGENCE, SLANDER, WRONGFUL INTERFERENCE WITH BUSINESS RELATIONS, CONCEALMENT OF FACTS, CONSPIRACY. All of these crimes were allowed in United States District Court for the Western District of Washington at Seattle, and in my opinion was condoned by the Honorable Judge Bill Silly.

I have always felt that, under due process of law, it was the right of all persons to receive the guarantees and safeguards of the law and the judicial process. It includes such constitutional requirements as adequate notice, assistance of counsel, and the right to remain silent, the right to a speedy and public trial, to an impartial jury, and to the comfort and security of witnesses.

After realizing that all avenues were shut off and I would never be able to appeal "pro se," I proceeded in filing a grievance against Greg Harley, the lawyer for Ratty, with the Washington State Bar Association in Seattle. I informed Earl of my intentions, and I received a letter from him dated July 18, 1999, pleading with me to withdraw the grievance. He said that two wrongs do not make a right. And he urged me to consider the words of the psalmist in Psalm 37.

This is the Psalm that he reads, and rereads when it seems like the bad guys won.

Even before I received Earl's letter urging me to withdraw my complaint against Greg Harley, I had already considered doing so. I received a letter from Nancy Olson, who is the Disciplinary Counsel for the Washington State Bar Association extending her regret for the bad feelings engendered in my case by the legal system.

On January 6, 1996, Ratty's used car salesman wrote a pleading letter to USA. He was begging them to respond to his plea for money due to the impact of Ratty's out-of-pocket the expenses they were having to spend on the extras. They were experiencing the same thing that Phoenix had experienced with out-of-pocket money to finance the extras caused by USA, and which did not include the extras caused by Ratty and their pre-cast supplier.

Ratty went on to finish the job with the aid of their bonding company. They were able to collect for most of the extras from USA, which amounted to over $250,000.00. I can now see why they had to get us off of the job, because my charges for Ratty's extras would have amounted to about the same as their claim on USA.

After putting all of the numbers together regarding our losses from this case. It amounted to over $500,000. Arnold and I recouped some of our losses on a few other jobs afterwards. We then retired Island Steel, and sold most of its remaining equipment.

On July 23, 1998, I received a letter from Earl Tiptop, informing me that he was no longer in the private practice of law. He had accepted a job with the City of Everett as an assistant city attorney.

Mary Ann and I decided to retire and sell our house at Lagoon Point. We weren't sure as to what we would do. We couldn't decide whether or not to move to the mainland, or remain here on the Island. Our grandkids wanted us to remain here on the Island, so that is what we did.

We leased for a couple of years while looking for acreage to buy so that we could build another dream home. There were several locations that we liked, but it was like buying a new car without the wheels. The property that we really liked was in Langley on Lone Lake Road. We made an offer on several parcels, but come to find out, the owner wanted us to pay all of the back taxes, so we declined, and bought a nice large house at Honeymoon Lake in Greenbank.

After a few years of retirement, I became very bored with getting up in the mornings, and not having anything exciting to do. I didn't want to go back into the steel business, so I applied for a job at Payless Foods, a grocery store in Freeland, as a courtesy clerk, and was hired. For the past two years I have tremendously enjoyed working with all of the wonderful people at Payless. My duties are to greet and bag the customers' groceries, and ask if they would like some help out to their car. Payless is a wonderful place to shop here on Whidbey. So if any of you that are reading my book, and have a chance to visit Whidbey Island, please drop in at Payless to do your grocery shopping and say hello.

Today is January 22, 2002, my birthday. My manager at Payless Foods, Tom Weasel Brown, has agreed to let me have this day off so that I can finish writing "Deep Regrets." Thank you, Tom. I am now 70 years old.

EPILOGUE

I would like to declare a few words of personal belief. My theory is that in this modern day we are all too tense and are living too fast. The exploding of atomic bombs which poison the air will, inevitably, have crippling results on future generations, the consumption of tons of tranquilizing pills to enable folks to deal with daily problems; these things were never intended by God to be visited on future generations.

Still, there is hope. I have told parent after parent not to give up hope, for help may be at hand. Remember, in this century the science of medicine has found cures for polio and smallpox. Tomorrow dedicated men and women may begin to find important solutions for the mentally and physically handicapped child, cures for diseases, an end to the crime of war.

Parents should never give up. If their child does not survive to live a normal life, as was the case for our beloved Christina, let the child bless their lives, enrich their lives in understanding, compassion and the joy that comes with serving the unfortunate. During the years of Christina's short stay with us; I never had the compassion for others that I have today. I was not privileged to know beyond reason that there is a Providence that governs all things. I have come to accept trouble and tragedy; because there's not much else one can do, but take it firmly and look beyond it, for we are made for triumph

There is little we can do to avoid the realism of "life and death," because they go hand in hand. We are all born to die! Because of my "Deep Regrets" in life, I have rebelled several times, both at my friends and at my wife and at my God. I have come to realize that it is useless to shake one's fist towards the skies when the trouble is here, on the earth, within one's self. I do not question God's plan any more. Man proposes, God disposes.

Today I know that affirmative thoughts create good things in my life. It keeps my body healthy, maintaining the normal functions of its organism. Our bodies must stay active so long as they possibly can. Though our flesh may be weak, our spirits will strengthen our minds to overcome matter. As I go about my daily activities at Payless Foods, I try to accept that everyone is created equal, certainly in God's eyes, but should be in our human eyes, too. I know that our thoughts need love. I believe the mind is sort of a perennial garden, in which our experiences are forever healthy and bearing fruit in the images and the thoughts we have put into it.

I have found that it does not pay to try to convince some people of all that I believe. But those people driven by imagination and intrinsic integrity will discover the truth of thoughts guided by love, and will begin to enact them in their lives. I am saddened by the work ethic of some of our younger generation. I find they do not to take their work seriously. They act as if their employers owe them a living. Little do some of them realize that their early work habits will remain with them throughout their entire lives, whether their work be good or bad. They should develop good work habits while their minds are young and eager, because good work stems from the honorable intention to do the best a person can do in a situation. Bad work habits result from finding excuses for failure rather than responsibility.

A child is always asked what he is going to be when he or she grows up. This is a question about work. The answer is usually something like, "Oh, I don't know." Maybe I'll be like my Dad or my Mom, or maybe a doctor, a Lawyer; or maybe, a Fireman; or maybe, an Ironworker. But most probably, we'll hear, "I'm not real sure." Work is applied effort in any endeavor. It is whatever we put our selves to accomplish. Whatever a person expects to achieve in life requires work. Work, in this sense, is not just what a person will do for a living, but what a person will do with his living.

Emphatically, I try to encourage young people to see the need for an education. The purpose of an education is to be led out from the narrower confines of home, neighborhood, or village. Education may focus on more specific ends, and can be achieved only by learning and training and experience. Education consists of understanding world, the environment and ourselves we live in and this can be achieved through by formal schooling coupled with lifelong experience. The five senses: hearing, seeing, tasting, smelling, and touching are the windows of our minds. They open us up to the world outside us and us to the world. We use words to express our thoughts, so we have to have command of language; we need to be able to manipulate numbers to build bridges, to balance our checkbooks; we need art, verbal, visual, aural to expand our imaginations. We learn from both those whom we love, if only we will see (remember my blindness to the answer, Mary Ann lived right under my very nose) as well as from our enemies. We learn from failure and success. Life is the schoolhouse in which we learn and learning is a lifelong experience: it does not stop until awareness does. As long as we are in contact with the world with any one of our five senses, we have data for learning. We have already learned great many things, even though we cannot remember how we learned them and then we have forgotten much of what we did learn. There is much we take on faith because someone we trust said it, like teachers, parents, friends, experts. No library in the world could hold all that we humans have learned as a species or, perhaps, even as individuals. But, learning is one of the most basic of all human needs and desires. Sometimes, it takes us a long time to learn this, "Living is learning."

Still learning ...

ABOUT THE AUTHOR

CHUCK HERRING was born during the depression years on January 22, 1932 in Birmingham, Alabama. He attended High School in Lenoir City, Tennessee, and served in the Military during the Korean War. He was wounded twice, and the holder of two Purple Hearts. He attended college at various places, such as the University Center of Alabama, and Fullerton College in Fullerton, California. He was the President of Island Steel Erectors Inc., for 18 years before retiring on Whidbey Island, Washington. He is the father of two children and the grandfather of 3. He has shared his life with his devoted wife for over 50 years, and still does. He loves to write, and continues his work ethic, part time with Payless Foods in Freeland, Washington, and loves every minute of it.

Chuck Herring
P.O. Box 1232
Freeland, WA 98149
360/331-6347
Lv2write@whidbey.com

ABOUT GREATUNPUBLISHED.COM

www.greatunpublished.com is a website that exists to serve writers and readers, and to remove some of the commercial barriers between them. When you purchase a GreatUNpublished title, whether you order it in electronic form or in a paperback volume, the author is receiving a majority of the post-production revenue.

A GreatUNpublished book is never out of stock, and always available, because each book is printed on-demand, as it is ordered.

A portion of the site's share of profits is channeled into literacy programs.

So by purchasing this title from GreatUNpublished, you are helping to revolutionize the publishing industry for the benefit of writers and readers.

And for this we thank you.